NICK FIEDLER

the HOPEFUL skeptic

Revisiting CHRISTIANITY from the OUTSIDE

IVP Books

An imprint of InterVarsity Press
Downers Grove, Illinois

InterVarsity Press
P.O. Box 1400, Downers Grove, IL 60515-1426
World Wide Web: www.ivpress.com
E-mail: email@ivpress.com

InterVarsity Press° is the book-publishing division of InterVarsity Christian Fellowship/USA°, a movement of students and faculty active on campus at hundreds of universities, colleges and schools of nursing in the United States of America, and a member movement of the International Fellowship of Evangelical Students. For information about local and regional activities, write Public Relations Dept., InterVarsity Christian Fellowship/USA, 6400 Schroeder Rd., P.O. Box 7895, Madison, WI 53707-7895, or visit the IVCF website at <www.intervarsity.org>.

All Scripture quotations, unless otherwise indicated, are taken from the Holy Bible, New International Version®. NIV®. Copyright ©1973, 1978, 1984 by International Bible Society. Used by permission of Zondervan Publishing House. All rights reserved.

Design: Cindy Kiple

Images: clear blue sky: iStockphoto
        man walking through a desert: Bellurget Jean Louis/Getty Images
Interior images by Justin Banger

ISBN 978-0-8308-3727-4

Printed in the United States of America ∞

Library of Congress Cataloging-in-Publication Data

Fiedler, Nick, 1982-
    The hopeful skeptic: revisiting Christianity from the outside
    Nick Fiedler.
        p. cm.
    Includes bibliographical references.
    ISBN 978-0-8308-3727-4 (pbk.: alk. paper)
    1. Christianity. 2. Fiedler, Nick, 1982- I. Title.
    BR124.F54 2009
    261.2—dc22
                        2009031642

P   22   21   20   19   18   17   16   15   14   13   12   11   10   9   8   7   6   5   4   3   2   1

Y   27   26   25   24   23   22   21   20   19   18   17   16   15   14   13   12   11   10   09

For Leslie, my wife and best friend.

In many ways, you are the coauthor of this book—

with an accompaniment of brilliant ideas,

inspirations and heaps of challenging questions.

Contents

A Note to the Reader / 9

1   Changing My Religion / *13*

2   Why I Like Agnosticism / *29*

3   Traveling / *47*

4   Flip-Flopper / *59*

5   Technianity / *71*

6   Scripture / *95*

7   Traditional Views of Jesus / *113*

8   Civil (Dis)Obedience and Revolutionary Change / *123*

9   Communities That Give Hope / *137*

10   Prayer: *Is There Anybody Out There?* / *149*

11   Conclusions and Concert T-Shirts / *163*

Inspiration and Insights / *171*

About the Artist / *174*

A Note to the Reader

I THINK IT'S FAIR TO SAY THAT most of the time we don't know the authors of the books we pick up. Buying a book can be a stab in the dark, only completely illuminated when we have made it a good way through the book. Starting out a reader might see a title like *The Hopeful Skeptic* and think, *Here is a book written by someone who has learned to live without knowing what to believe.* Then the reader would see the logo on the book's spine—IVP Books—and think, *Wait, this is a Christian book.* And then, based on the reader's thoughts on Christianity or IVP Books, she might either put the book down and quickly walk away, or decide to give it a closer look. And on closer inspection she might find that I don't fit the profile she expected me to fit.

As a way of introduction, I would like to offer a few notes about myself. First, as long as I can remember I have been intricately connected with churches and Christianity. I was raised in a Christian family, received a Christian education and worked in student ministry for eight years. So when I speak on Christianity, it is not as though I am talking about it from an isolated platform on the outside and picking on it. I am talking about it like I would talk about a close friend or a family member. I hope that if, at any point during your read, you think I am intonating something out of a divisive or hurtful spirit, you would give me the benefit of the doubt until you have finished the book and have seen the whole scheme of what I have termed "hopeful skepticism."

During the initial stages of learning about a ministry that my wife, Leslie, and I were considering joining, one of the leaders told me that a cardinal rule they held for all of their coworkers was to give each other the benefit of the doubt on every occasion. He was saying that if there was any situation where a coworker could mean one of two things in their words or actions, the rule was to assume that they meant the better of the two until you had a chance to discuss the matter with the individual. As a rule of thumb, this is a gracious way to go. It seems to be the high road, and though we may be incorrect at times, I believe that we will hold each other in higher regard if we can do this. I hope that for the duration of the book, if you can see two meanings or spirits about some words or thoughts, you will give me the same benefit of the doubt.

Finally, I want to make a note about my use of the word *skepticism*. I hope that the overall notion of skepticism within a faith tradition doesn't completely turn you off, especially because I do not hope to join the ranks of the popular modern skeptics. Rather, I want us to view the term and the ideas that come with it as a wrestling with God (like Jacob in the Old Testament story in Genesis 32:23-34). It is easy to see people wrestling with God, or with ideas about God, and think that they have got it all wrong, but instead of labeling these people as doubting Thomases, I hope that we can see skepticism as an act of wrestling with God—and, in that sense, being in close proximity to the divine.

Apart from this note on skepticism and my promise that I am not interested in being a church basher, I want to thank you for taking the time to pick up this book. It might not be the safest option on the shelf, but it is a journey that starts with packing bags, moving through my changing thoughts about Christianity and ending with a new appreciation of and way of approaching religion. I hope this book will become a conversation, because I would love to hear your thoughts on these subjects. These conversations have already started on The Nick and Josh Podcast (thenickandjoshpodcast.com) and my blog, The Hopeful Skeptic (thehopefulskeptic.com/blog). I invite you to join them.

1

Changing My Religion

I KNELT ON A COOL WOOD FLOOR and shifted my weight slowly from knee to knee to relieve the pressure that had built up under my body's weight. I have a smaller frame, even for someone who is six-feet tall, and my friends, family and various street people often call me skinny. But for that hour, on my knees, I felt like a lumbering giant. I felt overweight and tired. While I squirmed I started to feel guilty for thinking more about my sore joints than sitting in awe at the feet of the Tibetan Buddhist monk—a monk who had traveled thousands of miles to meet with a small group of followers that night in Atlanta, Georgia, and deliver a lecture.

Just before the lecture, the monk was sitting inside a private room, the one in which I knelt on an increasingly hard wood floor. My world religion professor at Georgia State University had pulled some strings with the local Tibetan Buddhist temple to allow me and three other students to have a private sitting with this world-renowned monk. He looked like a typical monk, wearing the bright orange and red cloth, the prayer beads, the overly thick Dalai-Lama-like glasses and having the shaved head, which looked like an aged peach with soft transparent hair barely hovering over the labyrinth of wrinkles. To the right of the monk was a man in a suit and tie, which somehow added to the monk's noble appearance. The suited man had been assigned to help the monk during his travel in the States, and he operated as a translator-assistant for our private assembly.

We were each allowed five questions, one at a time, straight down the line in a somewhat hurried manner. We sat and asked our very-American questions, wasting our time in the presence of someone who had spent over sixty years studying metaphysics, truth and ancient texts, and living ascetically according to his beliefs about ultimate truth. But we stumbled over the most pedestrian questions.

"Are those beads on your wrist, like, a rosary?"
"Why do you wear orange?"
"Are you just a vegetarian or a full vegan?"
"Why do monks sometimes set themselves on fire?"
"Do you always have to travel with a translator?"

We were completely unenlightened. I had spent my four questions (the ones about the fire and the rosaries were mine), and I was the last one to get to ask a question before the monk went to his lecture. I put down my paper and looked him directly in the eyes, trying to come up with something profound—something that would make the monk raise his head and tell me that I had attained enlightenment. All I could conjure up from deep inside me was, "I will never see you again, and you have devoted your whole life to understanding truth, what one piece can you give me today for my journey that will take me another step closer to truth?" (I used the word *journey* because it's a buzzword in spiritual circles and it can translate into interfaith discussions.)

It took a moment for my words to get translated through the suit-and-tie-man and into the ears of the older monk. He looked me in the eyes and smiled, but only to the extent an octogenarian monk would smile. Then he spoke directly at me in a language I couldn't understand but in a way that I felt the quiet rebuke. The translator too spoke very curtly, but I understood it wasn't intended to insult. The translator said, "You Americans are always looking for shortcuts. Asking this question is good, but there is no short path on a spiritual journey. I can give you no answer today; you have to walk before you can find truth. Go, walk and learn, and find someone to sit under for the rest of your life. Then return to this question."

That was it. The translator became a worried assistant who tapped his watch, bowed to us and ushered us out of the room to an assembly hall. In the hall we sat and listened to a ninety-minute lecture about metaphysics. It was somewhat gibberish, mostly about how we can know what is real, what it means to know and whether we can alter reality simply by changing our perceptions. I say it was gibberish because I didn't follow everything at the time—and the translator wasn't helping.

Two hours after arriving I picked up my shoes at the cubby near the front door where I had left them. I had a piece of paper with notes on it, but the only question I had was, Where am I supposed to go and learn?

That was five years ago.

IN THE BEGINNING

In 2008 a few major things happened in my life. My wife, Leslie, and I celebrated our second wedding anniversary, we both turned twenty-six and thereby entered our "late twenties," an African American was elected president, I changed my religion status on my Facebook profile from "Christian" to "Hopeful Skeptic," and my wife and I sold most of our possessions, quit our corporate jobs, packed two large backpacks and moved to the other side of the world on a journey that would last nearly fourteen months and span ten countries.

I guess that is a lot for one year, especially considering both my wife and I have college degrees and we had jobs that could have turned into "careers." We had never made such a big change in our lives before. The truth is, though, that that quick summary doesn't even begin to get into all of ways our lives changed, but it's a start.

It is also a good introduction to this book, which is born not only out of a podcast that I cohost with my great sidekicks Josh Brown and Josh Case, and our correspondent Ariah Fine, but it is also born out of a need to travel and change, it is born out of a faith that values skepticism, and it is born out of a global perspective.

Maybe I should start with the podcast. I am the cocreator and cohost of The Nick and Josh Podcast. (If you are already lost, a podcast is an Internet radio show, largely promoted by Apple's iTunes music store, but it is downloadable so that you can put it on a portable media device and listen to at your convenience.) Since 2006, Josh Brown and I have been podcasting on "faith, reason and absurdity." We have typically interviewed spiritual leaders, authors, speakers and theologians, asking questions that we genuinely wonder about. Sometimes the questions are deep and meaningful, like "Can you explain your understanding of atonement theology," but sometimes they are simple like, "What does the theology of Jack Bauer from the TV show 24 look like?"

The beauty of the podcast is that it allows us and our listeners to learn from some of the best and brightest people in emerging forms of faith and leadership. Doing this podcast has allowed me to learn about faith communities and meet people all over the world. As I was interviewing these people who lived further and further away from me, the podcast inspired the idea of travel. I realized that these people had different ideas about church and community, and I assumed this was because they were in places with different customs and even values. But I wanted to engage them where they were at—try their food, see their buildings, meet them face-to-face and see what about their surroundings make them come up with different theological ideas.

The podcast, though, wasn't the main catalyst that led us to travel; it just made it easier in some respects, giving us contacts all over the world. But the reason we ended up moving was because Leslie wanted to live overseas. She has always wanted to move overseas; she even told me before we were engaged. At first I fought with the idea: I didn't think I wanted to live in a foreign country. I was all about traveling, but living abroad, away from basic cable and the local Waffle House, seemed hard. But it turned out to be something that fit perfectly into our plans. Well, sort of.

Even now, Leslie and I consider ourselves newlyweds, mostly because we are lightweights with only a couple of years under our belts. We haven't gotten used to all the changes in our lives: living with another person, getting real jobs, figuring out what we want to do with our lives. That is a lot of stuff. And on top of that, we were trying to figure out our thoughts about religion and God. But because we both love to travel and were still early on in the life-changing world of marriage, we decided it was a good time to try living overseas—especially since we didn't have a house, a child or a dog, and Leslie's mom was willing to take our plant for us.

So we saved up for almost two years, living in a one-bedroom apartment with a torn couch and working jobs we weren't exactly enthusiastic about. (You know the mortgage collapse? That was me.) Don't get me wrong, our apartment was actually quite nice, but we would have loved an extra room and not having to work desk-jobs. Although the sacrifice would pay off, before we left for the other side of the world, we had ample time to examine our lives—mostly through the lens of our possessions. Even for a one-bedroom apartment and only twenty-six years of existence, we seemed to hoard an unimaginable heap of things. Our plans to travel for fourteen months made us realize that we had too much stuff.

Have you ever done the mental exercise where you make a list of the items you would take if your house started burning down? That particular exercise was a writing assignment in elementary school, and it instilled a fear in me of losing my house in a fire from early on. In fact, growing up I always kept a laundry basket by my bed, so in case of fire I could carry a lot more out of the house. I would have had some dirty clothes and whatever I could fit in the basket. During my childhood, my list consisted mostly of the dirty clothes, my inventions and some pictures. Imagine doing a similar exercise with what you would keep in storage for two years and what you would keep in a backpack to haul around the globe for over a year. This became a soul-searching time, but it trained us in the theology of stuff.

Do we need everything we have? No.

Should we keep everything we have? No.

We decided we should give away what others could use and save what was valuable to us, but then we had to think about what really was valuable to us. And we had to be prepared to wear the same six T-shirts and two sets of pants for a long time. We created boxes for giving away, throwing away, storing and traveling.

Then something happened to us. As we were putting our stuff into boxes and donating books that we never intended on rereading, we realized that a lot of the things we kept were only for filling space on shelves. For example, my bookcase was only a trophy case for books I had conquered; it offered me bragging rights to visitors. In fact, I wouldn't even put books that I hadn't read on the bookcase; I wanted them separate so that I could say that I had read everything on the bookcase. Things had gotten bad. As Brad Pitt from *Fight Club* had taught us a few years before: the stuff we owned, owned us.

But while we were packing, I thought about religion, about Christianity. And as I was thinking about my deep Christian roots and my impending travel, I thought about Facebook. So while I was updating my profile on Facebook and letting everyone online know that I was packing, I changed my religion. Right then—not under the pressure of the Inquisition, not while being dunked under water and accused of witchcraft and not even the week that I was fired from a church—I changed my religion while I was packing to leave the country on an exciting adventure.

Things were changing rapidly: boxes were getting packed, visas were being accepted, Homeland Security was tracking the travel books

we were getting from the library, and my views on religion were changing as I decided what to bring with me, what to put in storage and what
to get rid of. And while I was making those decisions, my own religious
beliefs started to get labeled and put in boxes of their own.

ARRANGED MARRIAGES

Religion is a big topic, especially where I have lived for over half my
life: Birmingham, Alabama. Some say this is the glittering buckle of the
proverbial Bible belt. I disagree. I think that there are other places that
would better be the buckle of that belt, but perhaps Birmingham is
the name "Bubba" that is branded into the leather of the Bible belt.
When it comes to the subject of religion, I think that my friends and I
are in arranged marriages—or at least we were until some of our recent divorces. This isn't the type of arranged marriage that my wife's
Indian friend almost got into at the coaxing of her parents. It wasn't a
marriage to another Indian who our friend had never met and, about
whom, the only information she had was the promised dowry, a
wallet-size 1980s glamour shot and an important last name. No, my
friends were in arranged marriages of religion.

Every single one of my friends that is or was religious became religious because of their parents. Now I am certainly not saying that this
is always the case with people, nor am I suggesting that this is even
the case for most. Obviously some children of atheists become religious and vice versa, but for my friends and me, this has been the rule
(with little exception) living in the Bible belt. Our parents had a specific faith, and we, in turn, grew up being told about the virtues of that
faith—and that faith only. I noticed that, by and large, my friends who
were Christians grew up in Christian households, and this pattern was
also true for my Hindu and Jewish friends.

However, most of the friends that I grew up with, even through college, were Christians. We were introduced to Jesus at a very early age
and told about his life, all of his miracles and about how he died so we

could have eternal life after death. We were also told about an alternative life without Jesus, which ended in an eternity of hell. With this little bit of background information, we were all led down to the altar where we said marriage vows to Jesus and put him in our hearts.

This isn't uncommon. I suppose this arranged-marriage thing happens in every faith: Hindus beget Hindus, Jews beget Jews, Muslims beget Muslims, and Scientologists, well, I don't know how they do it, but their children if they have the right thetan readings, will most likely be Scientologists. It happens to most of us in the same way that in an American school you are brought up with an American history book; it is just part of the circle you are in, and there is nothing inherently wrong with that. We teach what we value and what we know. And even though, sometimes, we completely turn away from what we are brought up in, a large number of us will follow what we were brought up to follow.

I don't intend to criticize the "relationships" that people have with Jesus, conversions to Christianity or faith traditions in families. I only use this relationship metaphor because a lot of Christians apply it to themselves, and they frequently use the metaphor when talking about religion. And I use this metaphor because, for my whole life, I have had a love relationship with Jesus. I sang him love songs, I trusted he would save me from hell, and I believed he was the only definition for the word *truth*. So I bring this up not to belittle the relationship metaphor but because, at the time when Leslie and I were packing and while I was asking all sorts of loaded questions about my religion, I realized that my relationship was an arranged marriage. I had been set to accept Jesus into my heart from birth, and in my churches and my Christian high school, I was given marital counseling from pastors and teachers on how to be a better spouse in my relationship with Jesus. I had been groomed for the position that I was occupying completely.

But after coming home from dinner with my wife's Indian friend, I turned my attention back to packing up my things. And I decided I didn't want to be in an arranged marriage. I wanted to date around and sow those wild oats. In other words, I wanted to ask a lot of really tough questions, I wanted to explore my faith from an outsider's perspective, I wanted to be able to doubt parts of my tradition that I couldn't blindly accept. I wanted to be around people that didn't blindly accept some version of scriptural inspiration because it was what they had been taught since birth. And I thought about Leslie's Indian friend, whose parents were giving her pictures of grown men in India, doctors and lawyers, but who had started dating someone of her own choosing.

Are arranged marriages really what happened to generations of the faithful? Did they ever stop to ask good questions to really get to know the faith they were being married into, or did they just accept the faith of their fathers because it was their father's faith? Don't misunderstand me, I'm not saying anything here about Indian culture and the role of arranged marriages (other than that I probably couldn't cut it as a traditional Indian), but I am asking if the same practice should be imposed on our spiritual journeys. Westerners have the hardest time accepting a foreign idea like an arraigned marriage, but when it comes to our faith, that seems exactly like what some of us have.

I really do want to stress how much I am not attacking Christianity or any religion, nor am I attacking my personal religious upbringing or any family for passing on their faith traditions to their children. But while I was packing those boxes for storage, I wondered to myself, *Why not pack some of those beliefs I have been married to for these years and suspend them until I get back? Why not try on something else for a while and see where I end up?*

So while I was logged into my profile on Facebook and was complaining about moving furniture or painting the apartment, I thought about what religion might best fit me, and I came up with the words "Hopeful Skeptic." And now, even after traveling thousands of miles, reading dozens of books and sipping tea with some of the most inspiring people in the world, those words have stuck. I can happily say that I have become a hopeful skeptic, and I invite you to hear some of the stories and thoughts that have changed my life.

Some of you will probably think that the religious label I have decided on seems to be a new dressing for the faith that I was born into, but I hope to show some categorical differences. Or some of you may say that I have drifted too far and I am now out of the fold. I understand that frustration, but I hope and believe that what I have become is more in line with the early followers of Jesus than the way I use to live.

THE CHURCH HAS BECOME A FLASHPACKER

My insight about the church, attained through my finite power of observation combined with my pretentiousness since becoming a world traveler, is that the church has become a flashpacker.

I don't blame you if you don't know what a flashpacker is; I didn't either until Leslie and I started traveling. I didn't even use the adjective flash as many people from the United Kingdom do, but you learn all sorts of things when you're traveling, like how to use waterless toilets, what various countries' definitions of the word *clean* mean, how to pack a years worth of stuff into one bag, how to accidentally rebel against the social norms of the country you are in, how to drive on the opposite side of the road and, last but not least, new vocabulary words. *Flashpacker* was a new one for me. It describes a backpacker who has chosen to have a more comfortable, cushy and "flashy" type of travel experience.

I should talk a little bit about the typical backpacker experience in case you have never been to a hostel to sleep in a room with eleven other people. As a rule, backpackers are crazy people; most of the people that we have encountered just up and left their countries without any idea of what they were doing. Some of the people we met left their countries permanently and could care less that their visas have expired (if Australian Immigration is reading this, the man you are looking for is camping in the Yarra Valley and is working on an apple orchard). These people come from numerous countries, they live out of one or two pieces of luggage, they camp in tents, hostels, minivans or just on the sidewalk to save money—money that they don't actually have. The average backpacker probably only has a couple hundred dollars in their bank accounts, and when that gets down to about twenty dollars, they find whatever work they can and do that until said bank accounts have enough to go see another city or another country. Backpackers scavenge for cheap food, alcohol and accommodation, accommodation that they usually share with a large number of other backpackers crammed together in a room with multiple bunks and virtually no privacy. Oh, and there is a lot of drug use, sex and awful European techno music. This is the traveling life.

Flashpackers, on the other hand, are typically a little older than the late teen and twentysomething backpackers. They are in their thirties or forties and actually have a job back home in their own countries. They save up their sick days and leave for more pampered traveling. *Pampered* doesn't necessarily mean that they are rich; it just means hotels over hostels, it means flying to places versus taking the incredibly long train or bus ride with livestock, it means seeing a country without having to work too hard to see it or be a part of it, or it means not having to work while you are in a country to fund the rest of your trip. It is nicer for the trip. No group showering or having to barter with the locals, and it is still traveling abroad by all means, but it is travel without all the hassle. You gain comfort but lose the spontaneity of getting lost in a place you don't know with scary locals. The latter is an experience everyone should have—often.

I think the church at large has become a flashpacker on the quest to follow Jesus. In the same way that both the backpacker and the flashpacker get stamps in their passports for visiting another country, the early church and the contemporary church are both genuinely following Jesus, but something is different. There was something to that first group. That group was scared for their lives, thought Jesus was coming back at any minute, met in houses, shared their possessions, had wild ideas about theology and had huge questions about orthodoxy.

There was something organic, dangerous and raw about them. Jesus was killed for trying to subvert the Roman Empire. One could even say he was accused of being a terrorist and that his earliest followers had that revolutionary taste fresh in their mouth when they met. But, slowly, that changed. Or maybe not so slowly. In the fourth century, Christianity became the state religion thanks to a vote of confidence from the emperor Constantine. When that happened, house churches declined and the temples of other religions became the new Christian churches. The state funded Christianity and it became a little, well, flash. Sure, it still gave money to the poor and took very seriously the teachings of Jesus, but it became domesticated. I would argue that it forgot the wild apocalyptic look that it had seen in the eyes of John the Baptist, and it forgot the hope of the coming kingdom of God that it had heard in the voice of Jesus.

Christianity didn't lose these things as if they never existed, but comparing the two versions of Christianity becomes like comparing the difference between backpacking and flashpacking. The backpackers and the flashpackers are in the same country, they are on the same soil, but some have started taking flights between cities, renting when they need transportation around town or booking prepackaged tours altogether. The tours are still exceptional, they are still lifelike, and you get some of same exact pictures as the backpackers, but as a flashpacker, you miss some of the subtleties of a country. You miss riding on public transport and sitting with the people; you only eat at the really nice restaurants and miss the hole in the wall that has authentic food. You don't get to hear all of the stories of the street people or the locals. You have a similar experience, and your stories will be great, but you miss out a little bit on something.

Again, I don't intend to bash flashpackers or the contemporary church. I have worked in and promoted the contemporary church, and I have done my share of packaged tours. But I think that there is a large group of people that are longing for forms and expressions of Christianity that aren't packaged tours, that aren't comfortable and that don't have everything perfectly figured out. These "backpackers" in the church try to listen to the voice of Jesus as much in its original context as possible, and they think the best way to do that is to hear it with as little preplanning, rehearsal or packaging as possible. They are often in Generation X or are Millennials, but they are also boomers and can run the full array of the age spectrum. Tony Jones calls them the "New Christians," and Phyllis Tickle describes this time as the "Great Emergence." Since Tony and Phyllis are much smarter than I am, I will just label them (and myself) as backpackers.

As backpackers, we are interested in raw expressions and new insights; we aren't comfortable with packaged deals. And though we find ourselves in a world of comfort, we feel the need to separate from that for periods of time in order to truly understand how other people live—but to also live wildly and with reckless abandon. It is possible to view backpackers as irresponsible and restless, and in some ways that may be accurate, but there is a part of the backpacker that solely longs for authentic experiences.

I won't run this metaphor into the ground, and like all metaphors it breaks down at certain points—the stage of development we find ourselves at as opposed to a general generational divide, and temperamental biases toward structure and historical precedence as opposed to reaction against obsolete cultural practices. Nevertheless I think it is useful—mostly because it shows two worlds that are very similar, but it also shows how the two styles of travel reveal different things about the types of people who decide to travel.

I see people all around me who are like me, we are traveling people. We love road trips or, as flights are getting more inexpensive by the day, traveling by air. And since English is being taught across the globe, it's fairly easy to make it all the way around the world with a couple thousand dollars and a dozen Lonely Planet guides. There is something that got kicked up in the dust of the Beat Generation—when the first road trip guide, *On The Road,* was written and when Americana was lined up on the side of every major highway in the forms of Cadillac ranches, oversized Paul Bunyan statues and large balls of yarn, rattlesnake pits, and world's fairs. We got addicted to traveling and experiencing new things. How long did we think it would take before it made its way into our worldview or into our thoughts about religion? We are backpackers, we are wanders, we seek authentic experiences, and we are looking for new expressions of faith. When we get the taste in our mouths, it leaves an ancient aftertaste, and it leaves a desire to go back to something we have almost lost.

2

Why I Like Agnosticism

BELIEF STRUCTURES ARE HARD FOR ME to get my head around. In fact, there are times when I will talk about many different subjects, and I will have to confess that those very subjects may confuse me. There are times when I will talk about many different subjects, such as Scripture or prayer, and I have to confess that the topics of Scripture and prayer confuse me. By admitting that I acknowledge that I don't even come close to having an adequate grasp on a subject, but I still want to interact with it.

Belief structures fall into this category. The structure of an individual's beliefs, particularly about theology, are made by interlocking singular beliefs together until they form a whole structure, which supports itself and stands together as a large, defined narrative work. Belief structures can be compared to a cathedral's huge, vaulted ceilings, which are self-supported, and above each building block is a small, narrative picture formed out of glass, which tells a story. Some are pictures of Jesus' birth or of Thomas poking Jesus in his side or of Jesus' resurrection. Each religion, denomination, church and, to some extent, even individuals live in a different cathedral of belief. But the cathedral of belief isn't just built with the Jesus story; it is composed of everything that we believe. Some cathedrals might not have a uniform look, but might be composed of a mosaic of different objects.

When certain groups want us to live in their cathedral of belief, not venturing into any other belief, we can feel caught in a power play. Sometimes we will pick a strict or rigid cathedral like this because it feels good to have solid walls around us, and maybe we felt torn between an all-or-nothing choice so we picked the cathedral of belief that specifically resonated with us more than the other. Nevertheless, for me in particular, when I am asked to abide in a belief structure that has been constructed by someone else, I get uneasy—regardless of whether the cathedral of belief was constructed with good intentions. I don't like being boxed into a prepackaged set of beliefs that seem to be set in stone, and I definitely want the freedom to travel around and visit other structures.

When I look at a faith or a denomination in a faith, I usually see a stable cathedral of beliefs. The beliefs usually create beautiful buildings, but sometimes I see stained-glass windows inside the building that support beliefs that I don't particularly agree with—or that, at least, I don't think should be etched into the building. I may like most things about a particular cathedral, but I may also want the freedom to amend its structure in the future. And that is why I like the spirit of agnosticism.

Before I move on with a loaded term like *agnosticism,* I want to make a few disclaimers so that you don't hate me and can feel secure in taking me seriously. First, in conversations about faith, I try to be as genuine as possible, even on topics that I now view completely differently than I did five years ago. I was being genuine five years ago with my thoughts about faith, but I also believe that I am being genuine now, even though my thoughts have changed. I see this writing as a continuation of that genuine pattern of thinking.

Second, I am not writing to persuade you. If you put down this book and don't change anything about your belief structure, I will not be offended or feel that I have failed. I am not trying to make you a member of my cathedral. If nothing else, I just hope to give you a tour and help you identify some similarities between your structure and mine.

Third, I am not angry at God, Jesus, Christians or the church. Many people write out of personal hurt, but I am only writing out of an excited and exploratory spirit. I want to learn and grow, and I encourage you to explore new perspectives as well. However, I change my views about almost everything, so if you don't agree with me on something, just wait a couple years. This book documents my current beliefs on particular topics, but I'm really just writing them down to start a conversation—a conversation I hope you will join, either with me or with those around you.

With that out of the way, I want to explain to you why I like the idea of agnosticism. I don't mean agnosticism in the sense that there is nothing we can know about God, and so it is worthless to devote our time to religious pursuit or even being part of a faith community. Rather, when I say I like agnosticism, I mean I love certain kinds of people under this large umbrella. It excites me that there are groups of people who don't claim to know absolute truth; there are people who center themselves on a paradigm that truth cannot quite be held completely—or even used like building blocks to create a solid structure. I like that, in a lot of these groups, the members don't hold "being right" as the highest priority in their thought, but they value the idea that they could be wrong.

I found out that I had a little bit of the agnostic spirit in me when my podcast cohost Josh Brown called me an agnostic while we were interviewing the man who was then the national coordinator of Emergent Village, Tony Jones. Tony responded:

> It's interesting Josh, that you refer to Nick as a[n] . . . agnostic. I would think that people would read my book and think probably that I'm fairly agnostic—in that there are a lot of things that I'm saying we just . . . don't know and can't know. And a lot of what

emergent has been about is trying to move beyond this language and tone of voice that communicates some kind of certainty about God and things of God in a world where I think we're all . . . becoming more and more aware of actually how little we really know, so I think I'm really agnostic.*

It was then that I thought the label could loosely apply to me. I decided that I liked the kind of agnosticism that is not driven by an anti-religious, anti-Christian agenda, but it is driven by the central thought, "I could be wrong and that is okay, but I would love to think it through with you."

If you took agnostics as a whole, I may only be describing a small percentage of them, but it's that percentage that I am captivated by. What if Christians in the world would at least concede a small parcel of ground and say, "I could be wrong on this point, and that's okay"?

There is a line from the Eagles song "Victim of Love," off the album *Hotel California,* where Don Henley sings, "I could be wrong, but I'm not." I love this line. I don't know why, but I have loved it ever since I found my dad's CD collection. It sticks out to me because it represents a dangerous, yet frequently taken, position: one where you appear to be able to give credit to the idea that you could be wrong, but in all actuality, you wouldn't give one inch on the subject. I believe this posture links up with some parts of the traditional Christian community. If some of us were to have a conversation about God, we might utter "I could be wrong," but it would probably be quickly followed up in our minds by the statement, "but I'm not."

What if our religious posture included a position of humility in our assurance? What would we lose? What would we gain? What would happen to our belief? Can Christianity still hold truth and salvation if it

---

*The Nick and Josh Podcast, "Tony Jones and the New Christians," episode 6.9, February 8, 2008 <http://thenickandjoshpodcast.com/2008/02/04/podcast-version-69-tony-jones-the-new-christians>.

gives up a little ground in a claim of absolute truth? Not that there isn't such a thing as absolute truth, but being human, we can't absolutely know it. Could Christians learn something beneficial from agnostics or Don Henley? I would say yes. Then again, I could be wrong.

WHAT'S IN A NAME?

Whenever I have a deep need for knowledge I turn to the all-knowing Wikipedia, and I search for the truth. I think Wikipedia works not only as a compendium of general knowledge but as a compendium of aggregated knowledge that works in an open-sourced kind of way. As I took an interest in the philosophical position agnosticism, I looked up the term on Wikipedia. Wikipedia gives about ten different types of agnosticism, and they range in meaning and usage.* In a similar way that denominations in the Christian church vary.

Reading through the definitions, I remembered watching the New Testament scholar Bart D. Ehrman on *The Colbert Report*. Ehrman said that he is an agnostic, and Stephen Colbert looked him square in the eye and said, "Isn't that just an atheist without balls?"† This is a good example of the typical feeling toward agnostics. The faithful and the faithless alike seem to both regard agnostics as wishy-washy people who won't make definitive statements about what they think. The typical view is that they are pathetic; they can't be bothered to do the soul-searching to make an informed decision. Somehow they get lumped in with the "lukewarm" who get spit out of God's mouth (Revelation 3:16). However, I think that categorization is a bit harsh, and I don't think the author of Revelation had my kind of agnostics in mind while writing. When I read Revelation I have faceless, faithless agnostics in mind that don't even try to think through their thoughts on God. I had to track down some modern agnostics.

---

*Wikipedia, s.v. "agnosticism" <http://en.wikipedia.org/wiki/Agnosticism>.
†*The Colbert Report*, Comedy Central, June 20, 2006 <www.colbertnation.com/the
  -colbert-report-videos/70912/june-20-2006/bart-ehrman>.

Daniel J. Boorstin and H. L. Menken gave a face to some of the early agnostics. Boorstin said, "I have observed that the world has suffered far less from ignorance than from pretensions to knowledge. It is not skeptics or explorers but fanatics and ideologues who menace decency and progress. No agnostic ever burned anyone at the stake."[*] This quip is used differently by atheists like Richard Dawkins, that evil doesn't come at the hands of people who don't believe in God as much as it does at the hands of the religious. But Boorstin seems to be defending his skeptical but explorative nature, instead of attacking another viewpoint.

While I like how Boorstin started to get my mind moving, I think H. L. Mencken shows more of the humility that can be contained in agnosticism when he said, "I tell you, if I have been wrong in my agnosticism, when I die I'll walk up to God in a manly way and say, 'Sir, I made an honest mistake.' "[†] Some might say that Mencken's in hell for his lack of personal belief, and I guess that the claim is debatable, but there is humility in being somewhat sold to your agnosticism while, at the same time, being willing to admit that you were wrong. The image of a man standing before God and saying, "Sir, I made an honest mistake," is a powerful and humbling image.[‡]

However, circling back to the Boorstin quote, he gave me a term that I like better than agnostic: *skeptic*. It doesn't carry the negative but it allows for space—space to explore, space to question and space to learn. Boorstin even follows the word *skeptic* with the word *explorer* to tie the idea to a sense of traveling or seeking. To Boorstin it seemed that skeptic and explorer is a linked identity. The skeptic isn't someone

---

[*]Daniel J. Boorstin, "The Amature Spirit," in *Living Philosophies* (New York: Doubleday, 1990), p. 24.

[†]Wikiquote, s.v. "agnosticism" <http://en.wikiquote.org/wiki/Agnosticism>.

[‡]I personally need to start making a list of "Apologies to God," because I know I have mucked up quite a bit and, worse, I have been unflinching in my mucking. There were points in my life where I probably would have told God he was wrong if I were to have seen him and he were to have told me a truth that differed from what I held to be true.

who shoots an idea down but rather approaches it with a different type of exploratory spirit—one that won't necessarily open-handedly accept something but also one that won't stop the impetus to learn more.

NAME CHANGE: THE HOPEFUL SKEPTIC

When I was starting to blog about agnosticism, I received a lot of feedback fairly quickly. Pastor John, one of my favorite voices of reason, suggested that "agnosticism has too much baggage," and where it gets a concept correct—that we can never completely know truth or God absolutely—it falls sort on other points, such as hope.

John is absolutely correct. If we land in the agnostic camp, though hope may be found, it is not inferred. And the other problem with the label "agnostic" is that people then assume you are not searching for any type of truth or morality, which is not necessarily the case. I don't think the search for God or truth is pointless. In fact, I am increasingly hopeful about the two. I find pieces every day that give me a brief glimpse into one or the other, and I love to collect these pieces and ponder them. I love to sift through history and ancient wisdom, and take what I think will hold it's own under close scrutiny.

However, this is a journey, and journeys are sometimes complicated. In fact this journey is a long one; it's similar to a journey in space: the closer you would get to a foreign body in space, the more you realize how far away from it you actually are. I admit that I get lost sometimes by some of the turns I make. Other times on this journey, I will have to cast away a piece of something that I held for so long, thinking it was a treasure and then realizing it was an old bottle cap. But isn't that part of the pursuit? Even if it is embarrassing that what you have been heralding as a treasure hunt turns out to be a recycling run, I believe the end is worth the hunt. If Jesus were walking the earth today, I think he would say something like, "The truth of my kingdom is like a retired man who sells everything he had to buy a metal detector and live on the beach"—because there is treasure out there, and it takes life-changing events to find every piece of it. But in the end it is worth it.

I think about a couple of stories about Jesus that collide with my thoughts on skepticism and agnosticism. There is this story recorded in Luke 22:36 where Jesus asks his disciples if they have a sword and, if they don't, to sell their very clothes to get one for all that is about to hit the fan. But in a bizarre turn of events, during Jesus' arrest one of his disciples who obeyed his teacher and carried a sword, launched a revolt by de-earring one of the arresting party. The very man that ordered the weapons immediately quenched the revolt and reproached the disciple for using the weapon. The loyal servant thought he had a perfect nugget of truth, but upon further inspection, for some reason his golden truth turned out to be pyrite.

It would be a cliché to say that the journey is the reward, but part of the reward in exploring faith is working through the process and taking in the journey. But the other part is that there is a reward when you find things that you can believe in. I think that being a skeptic can be a positive and hopeful position, and an enlightened one that puts everything into a refining fire. I would say that the place to live is in hopeful skepticism—it is hopeful in that skepticism doesn't overrun our lives or send us into a bleak or untrusting state, but it is skeptical so that our overzealous faith doesn't have us chopping off ears whenever we think we have something figured out.

WHERE AM I GOING?

In talking with friends of a similar age and background, it seems that we are moving toward something that isn't necessarily labeled as a traditional form of Christianity. But that does not mean it should be considered un-Christian. It is a just a different expression. It reflects an awareness that we don't hold the things of God like the church of the last thousand years held them. Whereas the traditional church stacks its blocks of truth to build high ceilings, we as hopeful skeptics are probably following the instructions of the band .38 Special: holding on to our pieces of truth loosely—but not letting go.

There are a few reasons that some of us have indulged this wander-lust. There are some in the church who hold onto views of Scripture that seem to run counter to the last two hundred years of textual criticism. Some of us don't necessarily believe leaders when they tell us that God wants us to go to war. Today we have more knowledge of early faith communities that had different traditions and beliefs altogether, and we are realizing that in the first days of Christianity, some of their initial theology was up for debate before it became the cemented foundation that it is now. So we've grown to question the form of the beliefs that have been handed down to us.

In addition, we are meeting our neighbors and finding out that other religions have stories and values that are a lot like ours, and instead of shunning them, we have great reasons to start dialogues and learn from them. The postmodern sensitivity that we have developed is probably from all that relativism talk, which is helpful for allowing open communication between people who believe differently.

Now I don't think postmodernism or relativism, as ideas, come anywhere close to explaining why I decided to start filling in the religion blank with "hopeful skeptic." The truth is that I don't wholly subscribe to either of those views. It isn't that I believe that every truth is relative or that I should put on the skepticism implicit in postmodernism. There are some reasons why I am skeptical, and there are things I am specifically skeptical of, which I'll spell out in the next few chapters. There are also reasons that I am hopeful and specific things I am hopeful about. But when I use this new title of "hopeful skeptic," the immediate questions that arise are Why do you not accept the label Christian? or What are you skeptical of? or What are you hopeful for?

These are wonderful questions, and I find the best religious conversations I have are with people who genuinely want to know my answers. I am not the first person who has wanted to distance him- or herself from the label "Christian," but I decided that I had to drop the label altogether and develop a space that would fit better and hold up to criticism. Instead of just getting rid of the label Christian, I wanted to define myself as something—not just define myself as non-Christian.

The first reason that I chose a new label is that I didn't want to represent myself in any way that someone would perceive as dishonest. I try my best to follow the teachings of Jesus. I believe that Jesus contained words of life in his teachings in a way that no one else has come close to. I think that his life and his teachings were divine, but when it gets down to some nitty-gritty doctrines, I have a lot of questions and I answer a lot with "I don't know."

Claiming that you don't know an answer that 90 percent of Christians believe is quite clear in the Bible puts you in a weird category. Most Christians don't know what to do with you, because they classify people by their beliefs. Beliefs are what make you part of the "in" group. They are what make you "saved" and "delivered." They are also what put you in a denominational category. But when you start saying things like, "I know that tradition views this doctrine one way, but I don't know what I think about it," then people don't know whether to think of you as saved or damned, in or out, and it gets sticky.

So instead of claiming to be Christian and wearing that label brightly—when there would definitely be some Christians who would not think that I am saved—I have opted to not use the word. That way I don't claim to be something that some people don't think I am. Using a different label is a way that I can be as honest as possible in conversations about religion. That being said, when I explain to many of the people I meet or hang out with that I am a hopeful skeptic, they just shrug it off and declare me an eccentric kind of Christian anyway, which is their prerogative. Nonetheless, I don't want to be the cause of someone else's identity crisis. And I don't have any problem with people who proudly wear the Christian label when they live like Jesus— which makes it an incredible label to wear.

HOW DOES A HOPEFUL SKEPTIC FORM THEOLOGY?

I know that some flinch at the term *agnosticism,* and all I can do is politely ask for the flinchers out there to accept the new term that I have suggested—*hopeful skeptic*—as a middle ground that is worth thinking about. Even for someone who is skeptical and hopeful, a theology of God that is based on hope can emerge out of what you may have viewed as a watered down version of faith.

I need to emphasize that the hopeful and the skeptical have to go hand in hand. I don't want to be thrown into the skeptics group altogether and then get blamed for not really being one of them. Nor do I want to stress the hope side alone and make myself only an Obama-speech lover. I use the two words together because I want to create another option, one with a slightly different theological perspective than the previous one that I grew up with.

To form more of a framework for how a theological structure can be built around this idea of hopeful skepticism, let's consider the tragic death of a youth in a faith community I once worked in. Whenever someone dies, especially a young person, questions start to circle: Why would God let this happen? or Where is God in all of this? Pastors and families who are trying to pick up the pieces try to make sense out of death by painting word pictures of heaven, but to me, their admirable efforts sometimes fall short during that initial time of grieving. When a roommate of my college friend died, a well-meaning Christian told him that Jesus had taken his roommate to a better place. My friend replied that the deceased was an atheist. Nothing was left but an awkward silence between the two then. What is a Christian to say to that kind of retort? Sometimes the Christian response doesn't play well in the world outside of the church.

The traditional Christian understanding that everything happens under the direction of God and for the purposes of God, and that we will go to a paradise beyond all measure at the second of our death, is very reassuring. But when in a group of religious and nonreligious, this well-rehearsed view of death is not always the most helpful script.

Personally I have never felt that it is my place to give platitudes or a nicely made promise of what heaven is like. For me, when people asked about the death of the young member of the community I worked in, they were usually expressing larger concerns: they were theologically conflicted with a picture of God, their worldview and the reality of the situation. At the time, I was skeptical of the traditional Christian script being the best approach, so I opted for a different angle, one that I thought would be more helpful.

Sometimes we need a different perspective and sometimes it is helpful to hear a few "I don't knows." In this instance that was my take on how to deal with the questions. I wrote a public response to the events with my thoughts on the situation, knowing that I could not honestly answer what God's plan was in all that had taken place—or even that I could assure anyone that the second a person dies he or she is in the hands of God. So here is what I wrote for the people that were asking me questions.

Praise the Lord he is the light, November 21.

I can't tell you exactly how the creator of the universe fits into an equation with a car, a trailer and one wheel that didn't come back on the road correctly. I truly wish that working at a church or being somewhat spiritual gave me insight to the master story being woven together and somehow orchestrated by a personal creative force. But it doesn't. I can't answer those questions. And when someone tries, they are going to come up short.

I do know this. The body of Christ is composed of a radical group of people who believe, among some other things, that the way Jesus prescribed to live really does make a better place on earth and lead us into something eternal. I also know that the body is most like Christ and most powerful when we serve and love each other.

I was talking with a friend of mine that was driving back from a concert he and his band had played on a Friday night. On their way back, there was an accident that took the life of one of the band members and hurt some of the other passengers. I listened for about an hour as he talked about his thoughts and feelings. I heard the story and my heart started breaking. I wasn't close with his friend that had died, but I felt the things he was feeling as he talked. I didn't say much, but after a while I asked him what he thought about God right at that moment.

He said the only thing that kept his thoughts on God positive was that, immediately, calls and e-mails came in from all over, even England, and they were full of thoughts of love and promises of continual prayer. I think what he felt was a community that Jesus had established 2,000 years ago.

I can't tell you how the creator of the universe works with a car, a trailer and one wheel that didn't come back on the road correctly —but I can tell you that the creator of the universe changes the thoughts of a heart to join it with a large community of radical people who follow a way that is not about themselves. It is about others, and God and building a better world through this love. And this community makes me cry over the death of someone that I didn't know too well, because I feel a loss in the community and because I feel the hurt of a community.

* * *

That response combines a little bit about what it means to me to be a hopeful skeptic and to create a theology of a hopeful skeptic. As a skeptic I find myself continually using the phrases "I don't know," "I can't tell you" or "I think it could be . . ." I use these because I don't want to wholeheartedly speak out of a traditional understanding, and at the same time, I don't want to push my current understanding as truth. It is not just about trying to be humble in my beliefs; it is about a serious streak of questioning that I battle on a minute-to-minute basis. I didn't draw on the promises of heaven, because I have no idea about heaven; I can only observe things with limited insight from earth, so that is the perspective that I used.

This kind of humility is a position that I observed recently in some amazing Christian leaders. It involves a communication style that I believe Jesus demonstrated. It is a humble voice, but I don't choose it out of humility, I choose it because I honestly don't know all the answers. And while I agree with the critics of questioning who might say, "If you only stand on questions you have a questionable foundation," that is why skepticism is only my posture but hope is my foundation. I have a great hope in the divine Creator, in the teachings of Jesus and in a tight community of hopefuls, and I believe that foundation will hold.

BUT REALLY, WHAT IS A HOPEFUL SKEPTIC?

Perhaps you are sitting there with this book in your hand, and at this moment, you are wondering why it is really important that I have dropped the label "Christian." Maybe you don't particularly like that I dropped it, and you wonder if it is a move that betrays the tradition of the millions who have followed Jesus from the time of his death. Perhaps you are classifying me as a "New Ager" or an "emergent Christian" or a "liberal." I understand the resistance, and my thinking fits into some of those categories in different ways. Perhaps at this point you would like to fit me into a category that already exists, or maybe, seeing some of these values and definitions together, you will respect the need for a new label, though labels don't always work well.

In some ways, I don't know why we need labels at all. I tried for a while to not use any, but that seemed to frustrate people even more than making up a label. We seem to need labels for things; labels help us in some ways. If we walked into a movie-rental store and there were no genres labeling the movies, we would be in the store a lot longer. Labels are helpful to an extent, but they can also mislead, and they don't describe things completely. Sometimes we pick up a movie labeled "comedy," which turns out to be more of a drama with the occasional bit of dark humor, and we feel misled. Love them or hate them, labels are all around us, and they are even needed for us to go about our everyday lives.

I guess my reason for creating my own label is I never want someone to think that I am a "drama" and find out that I am something else altogether. So "hopeful skepticism" is like introducing the "Sundance" section to a movie store. Those movies could be labeled a specific genre, but they are grouped only according to their acceptance at the Sundance Film Festival. To some it is confusing to separate these from the other genres. But in light of having such a limited scope of genres, it seems good to have created a new section altogether. So I have created a new genre, and I will try to paint a picture of what you can expect to find in hopeful skepticism.

Skepticism, in my mind, is about being highly analytical, being realistic, bringing the higher criticism of the Enlightenment and the modern skeptics into all facts presented to me, and being cautious of institutions and hierarchical leadership—especially ones that claim to speak for God—and questionable of any preestablished creeds of faith. If I were only skeptical, I don't think there would be much room for vibrant discussion—either with modern skeptics, who I don't represent, or with the Christian community, which doesn't always value skepticism outside the church.

As it is, though, I am hopeful too. That hopefulness brings with it realism that borders on optimism, belief that positive change in all aspects of life can be achieved, realizing the divine brilliance in the teachings of Jesus, being a lover of all good community and loving a global perspective.

A hopeful skeptic isn't quite the sum of the two, but I think it's close. To me it is someone who would rather make change than pray for it. It is about treating life and theology with a playful, creative and adventurous touch. It is about wanting to be on the forefront of a new, wide-eyed, wide-angled expression of faith. And it is about being a story collector, a story lover and a storyteller. It does bring with it its own labeling system, and some aspects of life and faith do end up being labeled "hope" and "skepticism." But hope and skepticism often interact quite a lot, and you find yourself switching from being skeptical to being hopeful quite a lot.

Is this different from your version of Christianity? Is it different enough that I wouldn't fit in your label of Christian? Maybe so, and I'm happy for you to label me however you would like. We as humans have a need for labels, so I don't blame you for sticking a tag on me; the truth is I would probably do the same to you if we met. All this to say, I think there is something to this hopeful-skeptic-type of person. More and more people that I am meeting don't like traditional Christianity, but they fit this description. And while I don't propose that faith communities come up with a creative new term for people like us, I do suggest that faith communities start changing themselves to allow for us travelers to exist within and around them.

3

Traveling

AS I MENTIONED, WE ALL TRAVEL—some of us on a microscale, as we are traveling to work or to go on vacation, and some of us on a macroscale, to the other side of the world every now and again. Some of us live within a fifty-mile radius of where we grew up, and then there are some, like my wife, who are part of military families that move around quite a bit. People who study these trends say that, due to current cheap and convenient travel, a lot of people live further away from their jobs than they used to, and more of the American population will move away from their hometowns then ever before. Plane tickets are at an all-time low, so many of us are finding moving away from family easier because it is not difficult and even inexpensive to get home for the holidays, and others of us find ourselves more able to fly off on vacations. I don't know that I travel more than my parents did, but it seems that we live in a more restless time. This restlessness doesn't kick up in the dust of our late teens, only to settle by our thirties when we have a job, a spouse and kids.

The restlessness that I think exists in our current day—if the number of jobs my contemporaries and I will hold in our lifetimes is any indicator of restlessness (I am pretty sure none of us are going to get fifty-year anniversary gold watches from our employers)—permeates all aspects of our life. So we travel, but not just for the sake of travel: we explore. The Internet helps us explore ideas and create relationships abroad. Sites like couchsurfing.com help hook us up with people (and their couches) from all over the world so that we can crash with anyone around the globe; this kind of site only works because we are open to talking with others, exploring relationships and exploring the world.

Travel has taken off not only as a hobby but also as an entertainment industry. The travel section in bookstores is lined with the typical travel nonfiction or books about a country, but it even has guides for every country. Lonely Planet, Frommers, Rough Guides and Rick Steve's guides can take up an entire shelf or several walls, depending on the bookshop of your choice. Travel even has its own channel on U.S. cable; we love to watch and plan our trips. So we do. I travel, my friends travel, and people in emerging conversations about faith travel too. And all of this recent travel has made me wonder if we are not only expanding our horizons but also our worldviews.

During an Israeli bombing of neighboring Lebanon, I learned how traveling could change my political and theological thinking. I didn't travel to Lebanon, but I used technology to bring Lebanon to me. I met someone through blogging that lived in Lebanon and had to flee his home because of the bombings, and Josh and I used our podcast to bring our conversation with this guy to all of our listeners. I was changed by talking to him.

While talking to him, I wondered about America's role in the Middle East and its political relationship with Israel. I wondered if this relationship has been because of promises God made in the Old Testament to bless those that bless Israel. Driving around Alabama, I saw signs on churches that said "Support Israel," but I didn't see any that said, "Pray for Lebanon." The interview and my correspondence got me to thinking. Now this didn't settle a Middle Eastern conflict or bring me up to speed on hundreds of years of history, but it helped me get to know someone who wasn't hand-picked by Fox News or the Israeli or Lebanese governments to speak on the matters. It also opened me up to the idea that by getting off my couch and meeting more people I could get a richer worldview and possibly even a richer theology.*

In addition, technology has made travel possible through online social networks, and technology helped create a relationship that changed me. It made me want to travel and meet people, and it made me wonder what aspects of my own theology might be similar to whatever it was in those churches that caused them to wholly support Israel to the exclusion of others. Maybe those churches were right, and maybe there were other churches with signs asking people to pray for Lebanon. However, what that experience and those signs made me think of was that I needed more interaction with people on the outside—interaction with people from Lebanon, people from Israel, people that live outside of my community and even outside my country. As backpackers travel and meet new people, do their worldviews change? And when they do, do their theologies change as well? I wonder the same for us as virtual backpackers.

As we engage more people, I think we see broader perspectives, and I think, through these perspectives, we are possibly engaging with new theologies. If it weren't for that podcast with a refugee from Lebanon, I would have never connected with liberation theology. The podcast put me on the phone with a refugee. Speaking to a refugee made the conflict real in my mind. And when the conflict became real, it made me want to understand it.

Understanding Middle Eastern conflict, and the plague of being a refugee, brings up the theme of refugees in the Bible. In fact, as I learned while reading about liberation theology, most of the Bible was written while the authors were in a territory that was either not their

---

*The Nick and Josh Podcast, "Sami Andraos," episode 2.6, September 20, 2006 <http://thenickandjoshpodcast.com/2006/09/20/podcast-version-26>.

home or not under their people's governance. I learned that, in this particular situation, the refugee from Lebanon had a life that was close to those represented in the Bible. In some ways, this guy fundamentally understood something much more than I would, something that the first readers of the Bible would have also understood—displacement, abandonment and exile. I didn't bring peace to the Middle East, but I was affected by new theologies that were brought to light while engaging with someone in the Middle East.

To boil it all down, cheap travel and technology are putting us in contact with all sorts of people that we would have never met before. And these connections will invariably affect our own worldview. We will quickly realize our similarities and differences with others, and they will surprise us. And this is a good thing. For us to help our neighbors (in a global sense) we must meet our neighbors. And for us to learn about each other we can't just learn about our next-door neighbors; we need to meet the ones farther off. Travel is helping us do that.

OTHER PEOPLE ARE LIKE YOU

Four months after living and working in Australia—picking grapes in vineyards surrounded by kangaroos, working for the government and becoming a construction worker—Leslie and I moved to New Zealand to live for nine months. After settling in, we started the long process of trying to get our taxes for Australia settled. It was a complicated process to say the least. I have a hard enough time getting my taxes sorted out in my own country, much less on the other side of the globe.

In Australia, we were taxed at about 27 percent, which took care of the regular income tax that we would pay but also included a superannuation fund, similar to a privatized version of Social Security. That superannuation was 10 percent of the total 27 percent tax, and we were entitled to get that 10 percent back when we left the country. We were told that the easiest and cheapest way to get our taxes settled would be to apply for the tax money due us when we left the country.

When we got to New Zealand, we started the process of making expensive phone calls, sending verbose e-mails with colorful language and filling out forms in order to get this 10 percent back—and it was only 10 percent of working for a few months. As you can imagine, though, there were quite a few hoops to jump through, but I thought I had it all figured out. The only thing I lacked was a copy of my passport, validated by a justice of the peace, as a proof of my identification. That seemed easy enough. I called and made sure that a New Zealand justice of the peace would do, and Brett at the call center of SunSuper assured me that it would.

I then took my forms and headed to the New Zealand post office and asked for a JP, justice of the peace; they told me that they didn't have one on duty, but there was a lawyer on the second floor of the building who was a JP. So I climbed up the stairs and walked into the lawyer's office, waited for him to get off a phone call and told him what I needed. Basically, all I needed was his John Hancock—or whatever the Kiwi slang for a signature is (Sir Edmund Hilary?)—on a couple papers, a two-minute task. The lawyer told me that he could do that, and it would take about twenty minutes. Red flag number one.

He then told me that he typically charges an hourly rate even for work that is under an hour. While this is assumed about lawyers and accountants, I was hoping we could skip the fee since it was just a signature. I told him that what I needed would hardly consume any of his time, and he agreed and said, "I tell you what, why don't you go to the shop, pick me up a twelve-pack of Heineken, and we'll call it even." This seemed fair enough. His hourly rate was $125, and I was sure the twelve-pack would only cost me about $18. So I left him the paperwork and headed to the store.

I picked up the beer and headed to the counter where I was asked for my ID. I flashed my Alabama driver's license, and the lady at the counter just stared at me. "I am going to need a passport." I remembered then that my passport was on the desk of the lawyer. "How about an international driver's license? It is a valid form of identification here." She got on her microphone and asked for a manager. The line behind me grew longer. The manager came over and said it had to be a passport. I remarked that I could drive in their country with a certain form of identification but couldn't purchase alcohol with the same ID. That didn't get me anywhere. So I explained that the lawyer had my passport in his office and that I needed to bring him the beer to get my passport back.

"Why do you have to give him beer to get your passport?" the cashier wondered.

"I needed him to do some work with my passport, and he asked for beer as a payment."

"Why would you pay a lawyer in beer?" Another good question.

"I don't know; I don't know how things work here. I figured you may still use a bartering economy for small tasks; it is a small town. How am I to know this is an uncommon practice?"

In the next ten minutes, I ran back to the lawyer, drenched in sweat, and got my passport back; then I went back to the store, bought the beer and came back for my documents, which I promptly mailed to Australia. After which, the company SunSuper sent me an e-mail saying that they would not accept a New Zealand justice of the peace's signature as valid authentication. Nice.

It was awful, but I learned a few things. The first is that, even in a foreign land and even though I was twenty-six, I still looked like I was under eighteen. Second, alcohol seems to be a universal payment system, not just in the American South but around the world. And last, I learned that government organizations throughout the world have the same reputation: the people who run the call centers will tell you what to do, and when you do it, it will turn out to be wrong.

Okay, so perhaps this isn't the most spiritual example, but basically, people are the same anywhere you go. You probably have some compelling stories about your travels when you realized that children from [insert other country's name here] act exactly like children from your home country. Or, maybe, as a female, your trips to Italy, Spain, Ireland and so on have led you to conclude that young men are the same everywhere—or that construction workers in any country will whistle at you. We are all similar.

These experiences are part of the traveling life, and if you haven't traveled or experienced the commonalities in humanity, then you've missed out on something big. When you're traveling, there are times when you'll say, "This is exactly what would happen back home," or "That guy is exactly like a Cambodian Josh Brown." Noticing that we are all similar is so important, but it is even more important that we graft the lessons of travel onto our theology.

If our theology doesn't accept that other people in the world are very similar to us, then our theology will develop into one that separates us and our view of God and truth from the rest of the world. And these kinds of "us and them theologies" breed forms of segregation. When we don't think other people are like us, we sometimes belittle them, their customs and their beliefs, because without this foundation of commonality among countries and people, it's easy to think that we have it right and other people have it wrong.

OTHER PEOPLE ARE NOT LIKE YOU

During a week in Tijuana one summer I had one of the most mind-shattering experiences of my life. Typically on trips to the Third World, a church group will build a church or a house for a community or a family. For the church group and for the people who receive the church or the house, this is a great experience. But lately, some people have been saying that the money spent on these one-week trips out of the country could be better utilized without having to buy twenty plane tickets and food and lodging for a church group.

But even though there is merit in the argument that we are spending too much money on taking trips out of the country to build houses, there is also merit in showing that these trips can so affect people's lives that their values, worldviews and spending habits are changed. This is what happened when I took the trip to Tijuana.

In addition to building a house, we spent a day at a camp where we invited all the street children from the surrounding neighborhoods to come and play, eat and bathe. For almost two hours I was in a small hut washing filth from children's feet, and something in me broke and was repaired all at the same time.

I take a shower every morning, which probably has to do with the fact that I was made to bathe daily as a child. In fact, I can't remember the last time that I missed a daily shower. When I worked in Australia I had to wait until after my construction work was over for the day before I showered, which was hard because I like morning showers, but I still managed one shower a day. I have no idea what it is like, personally, to live with limited water or without clean water. But the children that came into our hut hadn't been cleaned in months. They had dirt, rocks and animal feces all caked into their feet, and they lined up waiting to get washed. I sat on an overturned paint bucket for those two hours, just breaking, as I cleaned off the layers of dirt that had gathered over the months.

I now owe whatever degree of selflessness I have mostly to that experience. While I recognized that these children are just like children back home—taking every chance to spray me with water or snap me with a towel—I also realized that they are completely different. They are so underprivileged it sent my mind spinning, and I realized that the things that I worry about pale in comparison to what these children worry about on a daily basis.

Perhaps you have gleaned this kind of insight from a special on the news about impoverished countries, but to see it firsthand changes your perspective even more. I felt an almost-imperative command to keep these images in my head so that I wouldn't forget them when I was back home—wouldn't forget that there is a child who won't have a shower until the next group of Americans (or some other nationality) comes and washes them. When we experience the world in this kind of need, the world in turmoil or the world at war, we carry those experiences with us. So when we read a passage about Jesus speaking about "the least of these," we have an image in our minds, we have a name, and we have an urge to act. These experiences should change our theology. They should cause us to start reading the Bible differently. When we experience the gap in comfort of living, we realize how much of the Bible is about the poor.

One picture we see when we travel is that we are all connected and very similar in our basic humanity, but the other side of that coin is that we are still different. In my traveling, one thing that I learned very quickly is that I am not like other people. When visiting Third World countries, I noticed that I had considerably more than the people in those countries. Stepping inside of orphanages in countries like Honduras and Mexico, I don't know what has hit me harder: the smell or the fact that I am truly over-privileged when compared with a large portion of the globe. Something similar is true if you visit a country that has seen massive violence in the past decade; you realize that, even with the tragic events that have recently occurred in First World countries, other people are living in conditions different than you are. And if you have ever been to a country where females will not look a male in the eye, you will understand that there is a difference.

In the same way that we need to view humanity as a unified group of people, we need to understand that people have experienced and been shaped by things very different from what we have. We need to hear those words about Jesus mentioning "the least of these" and know that most of the "least" are outside our borders.

HOW THE TWO MERGE

With all of the nationalities and even religions in the world, there are countless ways that we are different and alike, but without the experience and some framing stories in the backs of our minds, when we read the stories of Jesus we will forget that there were the same differences and commonalities back then too.

For example, a Canaanite woman once came up to Jesus and asked for help for her daughter. Jesus responded that he had come for his own people and not for other nationalities; to this the woman responded "even a dog eats scraps from the master's table." Jesus was moved by her faith and healed the woman's daughter (Matthew 15:22-28). Now this isn't the only story of Jesus healing someone of another race or faith, but this particular one focuses on the question of whether or not the Jesus movement would be multiracial and include people different from his own. Jesus admitted that he had a mission that first and foremost included his own people, but then he strayed from that mission, amended his statement and healed the woman's daughter—recognizing her need and her similarity to his own people. Why Jesus didn't just heal her immediately, we don't know, but I think that the people around Jesus needed to hear the woman say that she deserved scraps from their table. In the same way, we who have plentiful tables need to bump into women like this and recognize as well that they deserve to be treated better than dogs.

All around the world, people have similar stresses, struggles and obstacles, and we become humble when we realize that we are not the only people in the world. Other people are like us. So while I don't think that Jesus made a multiracial movement so that he could sucker all the other societies into becoming more like his group, leaving the other groups without their own distinctiveness, I do think he chose to recognize the common threads of our shared humanity.

However, we must also remember that other people are different from us. Other people have different experiences, so we need to go outside our doors, our streets and even our countries in order to have interactions with people that will help us understand them. We need to do this because the majority of the world has less than we do, and if we can encounter them and see them face-to-face, we will realize that even though our day-to-day plans might not have included them, we should be like Jesus and let them change our plans.

There is so much that we need to learn about other people. We need to recognize and experience how alike and unalike we are, and we need to have those experiences with people from every religion in the world. We might do well to have open interfaith dialogues and investigate some of our traditions and beliefs that overlap. If we sat down in dialogue we could explore together themes of redemption and sacrifice that many of our religions share and our own understanding of these themes could be enriched by hearing an outsider's perspective on topics that we thought we had completely understood.

Many Christian faith communities have been able to have beautiful dialogues about what we have in common and where we differ from other cultures and faiths, and they are able to see others' similar humanity and act in ways that care for the different needs of others. But some communities have failed to take time to talk about what we have in common with faiths and cultures around us, so they only see differences that separate us. They can't get past the idea that other religions have it wrong, and I think those communities miss out on a more enriched community.

But traveling, which gets us more immersed in this theology of likeness and difference, helps us become more compassionate as we see our similarities. We also become more humble as we learn from older cultures and traditions, which is never a bad thing since it adds to our own robustness. In addition, traveling shows me how much I need to change, what I need to learn more about and what I need to be more humble about, and it gives me global perspectives that make me feel smaller and yet part of something at the same time. Traveling seems to be the perfect metaphor for my theology, because when we travel, we are in a constant state of change. Likewise, my theology is always on the move, becoming more informed.

4

Flip-Flopper

WE MIGHT AS WELL JUST GET to the heart of this thing: one of the biggest criticisms for skepticism is that it is not based on a firm foundation. It seems to waver and doesn't like to take a fixed stand. Well, I would like to take this criticism head on and just admit it: I am a flip-flopper.

In 2004, Senator John Kerry lost the American presidential race on a day that was victory for some and a crucial blow to others. It was a tooth-and-nail battle that ended with President Bush in the White House for a second term. Later analysis said that the loss could be narrowed down to two factors in this close race. The first was a television ad known as the "Swift Boat ad," where Kerry's military service was called into question by a handful of seasoned war veterans. The second factor was a term that was fed to the media and was used until it lost all meaning. That term, of course, is *flip-flopper*. And it was ingenious. The media could find early statements that Senator Kerry had made and find more current statements that contradicted his earlier ones. With clever prowess, they could apply both phrases to the Senator in a short clip to make the man look like he was two-sided on everything.

In our age of recorded, televised history, there is tape out there on most, if not all, of our elected officials, and it is quite easy to find contradictory footage (try searching YouTube for your favorite politician). Being able to record history and all a person's statements is great be- cause—given everything a person has said in the past, with all sorts of factors and contexts and facts varying—it is highly probable that his or her statements and thoughts will eventually change.

Imagine if everything you ever said was recorded. Scary isn't it? If we were so inclined, we could record almost anyone. Take the exam- ple about Jesus instructing his followers to take up arms. Now imagine the following would-be political ad:

(Fade in from black and a slow-motion Jesus stands in a robe, with his hand outstretched; a man with a deep, ominous voice narrates.)

Narrator: "Jesus of Nazareth looks tough when he is talking to his
             friends."

(Insert white text on a black background, quoting Jesus saying that the disciples should not only have one sword but also get two.)

Narrator: "But when one friend tries to save Jesus on the night of
             Jesus' arrest, he chastises his friend."

(Cut to a picture of an ear in the dirt.)

Narrator: "Do you really want to follow someone who can't make
             up his own mind? Flip. Flop. This ad was paid for by The
             Citizens for a More Roman Empire."

See, we can do this almost anywhere, with nearly everyone. Now while it would be fun to do this with a lot of different Scriptures and biblical figures, I will instead apply this to my own life and theology.

On my eighteenth birthday I headed to my local tattoo parlor with my good friend Clint, and I joined the ranks of the brotherhood-of- the-tattooed. My first piece of ink was the Greek word *xenos* on my left, inner forearm. I had learned in my Bible class at my Christian high school that it meant "alien, stranger or foreigner."

The author of the New Testament book of Hebrews used this par- ticular Greek word to describe Abraham who, in response to a call from God, left his homeland to take his family to a place that God would show him. The author of Hebrews stated that Abraham was blessed because he did not claim the earth as home, but rather Abraham felt that he was an alien or a stranger and believed that he would inherit a spiritual or heavenly home.

When I got *xenos* tattooed on the inside of my left arm, I strongly believed that nothing on or about earth mattered. I believed that the earth was as damned as the unsaved people on it, and the only thing that mattered was getting to heaven and getting other people to heaven with me soon since it was all going to burn. So I had a word carved into me to remind me that I had nothing to do with this world. I was only a stranger here, an alien, waiting to get off this God-forsaken planet as fast as possible.

THINGS CHANGED. MY THEOLOGY CHANGED. FOR THE BETTER.

Now, I still love my first tattoo, and the script is very well done, but I interpret it quite differently now. My worldview now accommodates a deep appreciation for the created world and for our time here. I believe that what we do here matters immensely, and not just the soul-saving bit. My goal in telling you this isn't to get you onboard with my worldview; it is only to admit that I am a flip-flopper and that fact is written in ink.

Maybe people will start selling flip-flops with my face on them, like they did with Senator Kerry, and that's okay since I would buy a pair. Even if people levy an attack against my spirituality, that's okay too, because I learned something: People change. We all change, and it happens frequently.

When I was blogging about flip-flopping, years after getting that tattoo, Clint reminded me that the ability of humans to change and adapt is possibly one of our greatest survival tactics. Humans—better than any other creature—can learn, adapt and change with ease. Clint is right, and because of that adaptability, what I think now will be different from what I will think in nine years.

There is a humility that needs to exist inside religious beliefs—a humility that I think I took on with the "skeptic" side of my label. Without humility we are doomed to be one-sided, exclusive, fanatical and perhaps militant. Humility is what I view as the healthy form of skepticism, and because of this humility and a bit of skepticism about the absolute correctness of our personal theology, we can escape embarrassment when our flip-flops are detected.

So maybe we should never get a belief tattooed on us, physically or metaphorically, unless we are completely ready to say at a later date that we were wrong before. As for me, I can admit that I have changed, yet I can also say that I still feel like a stranger in a strange land—especially when I am in the Bible belt. My focus has changed from the far-off afterlife to the close-up, changeable, abundant life.

Just like a critic of agnosticism might say that if you don't stand firm for something, you will fall for anything; the critic of flip-floppers might say that if we view our faith as something that's changeable then we don't have a strong faith. A similar argument has been made to me when I've asked Sunday school teachers if you can lose your salvation. The majority of the time when I've asked this question, I've been in one of two denominational camps: Southern Baptist or Presbyterian. Neither of these camps believe that you can lose your salvation—or, more specifically, none of the affiliated churches I was in at the time held that belief. They did have one caveat though: if you lose your faith, it is because you never had a real faith to begin with.

I've always thought that this is a beautiful shuffle of the feet. What the teachers have done is acknowledge that the denominational stance is to believe that you cannot lose your salvation; however, they have allowed for an out by claiming that you may not have ever actually let God in. This way, when we seem to flip on our decision for salvation, there are those who would say that we never made a firm decision at the start.

Can there be truth in this idea? Certainly a lot of theologians have thought this to be the explanation, and I suppose this is a plausible way to think about belief. However, there is another way that I will suggest, and that is that we are flip-floppers. We change, we shift, we learn, we adapt. We are not the same yesterday, today and forever. If we were, then we would never have had any scientific or technological breakthroughs, and we would not be able to be classified as even a simple form of bacteria.

It is possible that the same people who were vitally involved in their local churches, and believed every doctrine of those churches, have been thinking through some different forms of theology and have tossed out some old theologies. However, instead classifying these people as unsaved or backsliders, we need to acknowledge that these people, like all people, have changed over time. So we can take the low road and label them as flip-floppers, or we can take the high road and give these community members the benefit of doubt, realizing the truth about humanity is that we all will morph—and that should happen in our theology or else our religious beliefs will fail in the next couple hundred years. They will fail because society is constantly changing and we are constantly facing new things. We are always on the cusp of learning something that changes an old thought, even in the field of theology. This has happened with the fossil record, archaeology, evolution and astronomy. We have stumbled onto ideas that have changed our old views, even the views that we thought were supported by the Bible.

CHARACTER

Jeremy is one of my close friends. He and I worked in youth groups in the same city for a few years, and we would meet at coffee shops or pubs to talk about our lives and our thoughts about God. Invariably, one of us would eventually mention ways that we thought we had completely dropped the ball in the past week—whether at work, in our relationships or whatever. He came up with something that he would say about a person's character, and I think this also applies to flip-floppiness: "Your character is never defined by one act." What he was suggesting is that our character cannot be measured by a single event, good or bad; it is measured in the long term.

This is an inspiring thought for me, and I'm guessing it could be for you too—especially if you have ever done something stupid at some point in your life. Our lives are much more intricate than one action; in fact, at no single point in our lives could we possibly be completely defined.

So what if we viewed our own thoughts and firmly held doctrines with that in mind? What if, instead of being on the brink of dying for a doctrine, we admitted that this one thought we have about theology is not the thought that defines us? I am not saying that we have to allow for a change in God, just our view of God. What if we could put off defining ourselves until a later date, in order to see how we've been shaped on the whole by our thoughts and beliefs? What if we could give ourselves space in the future to amend our theological ideas? In this way, we would never define the whole of ourselves on a single point of doctrine at a single moment in time.

For example, if I decide that some scriptural doctrine is only defined a single way—such as my view of atonement or the position of women in the church or salvation or the second coming or baptism or worship and so on—then I will want to live the rest of my life in keeping that view, and if I change or am confronted by new interpretations, I will be reluctant to change my mind, because I have stuck myself to one way of thinking.

A similar maneuver can happen in rock climbing, where you can climb to places that you can't climb out of. You can get yourself to a hold or a ledge, but you find that once you are there, there isn't an easy way out. You may even get stuck there for a quite a while. I think of working through doctrines like rock climbing, and I don't ever want to get myself stuck in a spot doctrinally that I later decide I don't want to be. While I see theology as a great climb, I am cautious in each hold. But I am not so cautious that I would ever stop climbing out of fear of getting stuck on a ledge, yet I do want to be wary of what I latch on to and leave myself another grip. Every hold we grasp onto has the potential to help us with a climb or get us to a place we don't want to be.

I propose defining the spiritual life on a broader scale than just a small, single hold—a scale broad enough that it will give us room to pick several holds or even change holds so that we don't get stuck. And I also propose that we recognize that the scale is so large that there isn't just one rock face. There is a lot of climbable rock out there. Instead of defining our faith on the little bits that we might need to let go of, it would be better to define our faith based on the strongholds that are steady enough to grasp or stand on but will allow us to keeping moving up the rock face. For example, Jesus proposed a broad definition: love the Lord with everything and love your neighbor as much as you love yourself (Mark 12:30-31). I can't imagine that this kind of hold might be a bad hold. The command opens up for us all sorts of places to climb to. It is not a confining ledge, but a great stepping stone. Stepping off a stone like this one enables us to move up the rock face, exploring positive possibilities. However, when we hang tightly to a specific doctrine that is completely defined, we could end up stopping the climb. When we use a hold like loving those around us, we have a lot to build on, but if we try to narrow it down and define specifically who our neighbor is, we are moving toward getting stuck.

As much as we'd like to, we can't know everything about God. We are continually learning more about him, so a broad statement of beliefs will help us climb upward, off of certain basics. Even if we have to backtrack at certain points, we are constantly climbing toward knowledge about God. And this is the value of not holding onto certain doctrines too tightly: we give space for people to change their minds, or flip-flop. For example, by not holding too tightly to particular doctrines, we have room for the member of the congregation who changes his or her mind on a specific doctrine, and we don't cast the person out of the body all of a sudden. Rather, he or she is still under the blanket of the congregation yet free to change and adapt in light of personal reflection. This isn't to say that he or she is right or wrong on the subject. Maybe we think so, but that doesn't mean the person shouldn't be allowed to work through his or her theology or no longer have the support of a community to work through important beliefs. We need to let God work in people and allow members of our community to climb. We need to give them the freedom to find holds that will work for their betterment, never forcing them to stay on a ledge or backing them into a hard spot—because that spot might not be right or it may not help them move to a place where they can learn more about God.

This is not to say that our faith communities shouldn't hold beliefs or that they should remain silent when someone in the community is expressing divisive thoughts. But in their beliefs, our communities should allow for the change that is in all people. In each one of our statements of belief, we should ask if the points are helping us foster more conversation on the topic—to broaden our understanding of why we believe what we believe—or if the points are asking people to stop climbing when they come to certain topics.

Admitting that humans change is the first step toward giving ourselves room to grow. And if we accept that we all change, then not only are we open to correction but we don't beat ourselves up when we or our beliefs change. There is a beautiful quote by Reverend Charles Kingsley after reading Charles Darwin's *On the Origin of Species*, he said "It awes me. If you be right I must give up much that I have believed."* Perhaps Reverend Kingsley's religious peers would have labeled him a flip-flopper, but didn't he just adapt to new information available to him and make a decision based on that information?

---

*Melvyn Bragg, *12 Books That Changed the World* (City, U.K.: Hodder and Stoughton, 2006), p. 137.

If we can accept that we all will change, and if we can accept that change is an integral part of life that happens in all our bodily processes, then we are moving toward the unification that Jesus spoke about. I hope we get rid of the terms or phrases like *flip-flopper, backsliders* or *never really saved,* as well as all the other ways we malign and label people who change. I think we ought to take some time to thank God that the theology of slaveowners and women haters has changed, and we should pray that we will change where we need to. And if we have to use flip-flopper, let's just reserve it as a self-effacing reference to ourselves.

In the movie *Dogma* Rufus, supposedly the thirteenth (and only black) disciple suggests that "ideas" are preferable to "beliefs." His argument is that you can change an idea, and people won't kill or die for an idea the way they will for something labeled a belief. Hearing Rufus elaborate on that aspect of religion and theology was one of the most spiritually enlightening events of my life. Because we are all flip-floppers, so why not just label our beliefs "ideas"? That would make it easier for us to hold onto them in a way that would allow us to change them if we get new information at a later time, and it gives us plenty of space to have "new" ideas.

OUR HEADS AND CHANGES

While thinking about my own ideas, I happened on a group of books called the One Guy's Head series by Don Everts. Don describes his mind as a huge dorm or a shared house, and his individual ideas are the people that dwell together in that communal abode. Don walks through how each of the tenants (ideas) interacts, and he shows what the process of new ideas moving in entails and what house/dorm conversations, debates and fights look like.

Ideas and beliefs seem to operate in our heads much like Don suggests. They are all residents in our minds. For most of us, our tried and true doctrines are the permanent residents of the house, and when new and improved ideas come along, they may gel with the older housemates or they might not. And when the two ideas conflict, someone has to leave.

If we entertain this metaphor of our minds being a shared house and our ideas being the tenants, we might be able to better understand people who seem to flip-flop. So instead of seeing people around us who have changed their beliefs as "loopy" or "unsaved," we can see them as having all sorts of ideas living in their minds. And if we were to give these people the benefit of the doubt, as people who wouldn't just kick someone out of the house willy-nilly, we might see that a lot of thought has gone into who gets to live in the house. There were probably good interactions with the new guy (idea) and great debates with the old guy before the owner finally decided that the old guy would have to go in order to make room for the new guy.

Maybe this is confusing, so let me put it another way. Let's say you have a neighbor who is a good friend that you have known for years, and now she's talking about having some friends move in. Then, after some time, she tells you that she can't really talk about it, but she's had to ask her friends to leave, having decided that it just wasn't such a good living arrangement. I doubt that you would assume that your friend is crazy for deciding she shouldn't live with these other people. Rather, you would probably trust her judgment and even console her by saying that it is hard to change living conditions and it doesn't work all the time. Being a close friend, you wouldn't suggest that she is a flip-flopper; in fact, you may even think that she was admirable for trying to entertain some other friends.

I think we should operate the same way when we have friends that let new ideas move into their heads. I think part of being a community of believers is not just believing in God together, but believing in one another as a community of which God is a part. And to go further, that being part of that community of believers is to believe in the members of the community. We should trust that the community members think critically about their beliefs and have a good set of criteria for who they let live in their heads. And we should understand that ideas might move in and out. This isn't to say we can't make suggestions about the tenants (ideas) that we saw were awful tenants, leaving stains on the carpets and holes in the walls, but we should view our minds (and our neighbors' minds) as dynamic, understanding that our beliefs will reflect our changes from time to time.

5

Technianity

IN THE INTEREST OF FULL DISCLOSURE, I should admit that I am a huge techie. I spend a good bit of my time reading about technology and computer-related innovations. Some of you may think that this chapter will be too computery, but I think it is a good way to explore the sort of things that I would put in a box marked "skeptical." Being that the technological revolution is alive and well, I think technology is pertinent to our theology and the way our faith communities work—I am concerned with models of leadership and community that don't fully embrace the technological revolution.

The Internet was born in the way most powerful world-changing devices are born: deep inside a military complex. Most of us technophiles know the story of ARPANET becoming the giant, global network that it is today. With no head of operations or single mainframe to support it, the Internet is a series of connected hubs and hosts of data. And you may or may not know, but a great deal of the Internet has evolved largely because of the porn industry. (Wow, my spell check didn't even try to correct the word *porn,* which should tell us something.)

The porn industry has always been looking to get immediate content to anonymous users. In part, if we love the Internet we must understand that a good deal of the technology is possible due to the great investments made by the porn industry.* I guess it is similar to the way that Christianity became mainstream due to its acceptance by Constantine and the institutional machine.

However, regardless of what propels the technology of the Internet or what established Christianity into culture, they now both exist in close proximity, and they can't help but bump into each other (in other ways than just that there are men who are addicted to Internet porn and there are ministries to help them). In today's world, or more accurately in today's affluent world, everyone is online. I e-mail my grandmother, I talk to my mom on Facebook, and I blog to whoever cares to read my random thoughts. And I'm not the only one. The number of people who have mobile phones or have access to the Internet is staggering. Even when I'm traveling in Honduras, Cambodia, Nepal or the Dominican Republic, I see plenty of mobile phones and Internet cafés. And though their speeds may be sluggish compared to my connection at home, in most countries except China, anyone can get every webpage that I can.

UNIVERSAL EQUAL ACCESS

In 2008, Nicholas Negroponte launched One Laptop Per Child, or OLPC, with the aim to get a laptop in the hands of every impoverished or underprivileged school child possible.† Though the success of this effort is debatable, it did get these inexpensive laptops out there, and other companies joined the fight to get affordable laptops on the market. There are now all sorts of companies sprouting up to get technology and the Internet out to as many people as possible; in fact, that is one of the main values of the mega-search engine Google.

---

*Brooke Gladstone, "Is Pornography Driving Technology?" *All Things Considered,* November 29, 2002 <www.npr.org/templates/story/story.php?storyId=861968>.
†See <http://laptop.org>.

The largest impact of the Internet could very well be that it is providing the world with unlimited access to information and that it allows user content to be hosted globally. With sites like Wikipedia you can not only access facts about any topic you can think of, you can also access collective facts about a topic. For example, not only is there a standard encyclopedic explanation of your topic but users have also combined their knowledge of the topic to provide a groupthink definition. Then people can debate or vote on the accuracy and objectivity of the additional information. In New Zealand I met a girl whose college professor let her use Wikipedia as a quotable source for her research (much to the chagrin of other academics and the delight of techies).

Besides websites like Wikipedia that present definitions of topics, there are aggregator sites like Digg <http://digg.com> which display what web content is getting the highest rating by users. Some scandal published on the *Wall Street Journal* website gains traction as Digg users share, or "Digg" it, and its ranking on digg.com gradually goes up. Users can even create a personal Digg homepage to display their topics of interest. My Digg page knows that I am interested in technology, religion, world politics and great YouTube videos, but it knows not to show me anything about sports.

In addition to the massive amounts of information accessible with the web, the web is also a new sort of community. Global interactive communities can match your every interest with the interests of others like you. For example, if you want to find other Dungeons & Dragons players who like to roll their twenty-sided die while listening to the group Rage Against the Machine, just search for it. Didn't find it? Then make your own group, and within a few days you will find others from everywhere.

But what does any of this have to do with Christianity and skepticism? Quite a bit. I think I am cautious about the old structures still in place in some Christian institutions because of these new online communities. Here is how I see it: for a majority of the time in the church's history, the congregation has been kept outside of the theological and historical body of knowledge. I believe this developed from eyewitnesses giving accounts to others and then it morphed into the educated presenting information to the uneducated, and during this transition the congregation, the laity, was kept out of the know.

During the first century there were the people who had seen Jesus and those who hadn't. The eyewitnesses who had seen the events were the apostles, and they spread the good news by word of mouth. The listeners would then spread the stories as they heard them. Scholars tell us that a few decades after Jesus' life, the stories were collected and written down to be read in congregations, along with letters from people like the apostle Paul. Eventually the written Gospels and these letters became the scriptural canon. But copies of Scripture were limited, and those who could read were in the overwhelming minority. So a trained clergy developed to lead the congregation, and to use their own understandings to give the information from the canon to the laity.

By the time of the printing press, the clergy had great institutions of learning and the congregations had largely been cultured to listen and to use the pastor/clergy/pope as the source of truth regarding all things spiritual. The laity wasn't cultured specifically in a bad way, but they were cultured out of necessity: they hadn't been able to read Scripture and didn't have the schooling to tell them what to do with Scripture, so the laity left that to the clergy. Most of the time the clergy did a good job respecting the authority they had been given. At some points, though, this knowledge of the few was misused, and it seemed as though some leaders wanted to keep the laity in the dark. Such seems to have been the case with Pope Gregory XVI, who banned railways to keep out foreign influence on Christianity.*

But we don't have a papal ban on railways, and in most countries literacy rates are higher than they have ever been. The literate are no

---

*Encyclopedia Britannica online, s.v. "Gregory XVI" <www.britannica.com/EBchecked/topic/245693/Gregory-XVI>

longer in the minority, and now we can get out information from the Bible itself—and also from books we pick up or devotionals about spiritual topics. But sometimes even our readings don't push us too far from our clergy's teaching, because many of the books we read are from a curriculum from our church or from our church's bookstore. In some ways, what we read is still under the umbrella of our leaders' influence. Not in a crazy *1984* way, just in a way that has the potential to keep us in the same thought process of our church leaders. And while this might not be an accurate generalization for every church, I think it is safe to say that the majority of churchgoing Christians who read Christian literature will read what is accepted by or provided in their home churches. We trust our churches and we trust our churches' libraries, because our churches and leaders have earned our trust—they haven't been forced on us via a state church or a national religion.

Thanks to the technological revolution, though, our understanding of Christianity is broadening. For the last two hundred years, biblical scholarship—the information that we have about the origin and meaning of Scripture and the history of Jesus—has taken off. Typically this information was extremely academic and not used in the pulpit, but the Internet has quickly filled with accessible information about the historical Jesus, early Christianity and early church doctrines. Most of the world found out that the Internet was full of this kind of information after *The Da Vinci Code* became an international bestseller. There was an interesting purchase base of this book, and though it wasn't in the church bookstore, it made it into the hands of a good percentage of church people. Readers rushed online to look up facts and flaws. Why? Because we flew through that short-chaptered book, and getting online was much faster than waiting for a sermon series or a book to refute it.

Or maybe we thought that our pastors might not give us all the angles or know everything about ancient Christianity or religious texts. To be fair, most of us have never heard our pastors speak about the Sacred Feminine, the Knights Templar or other Gospels, but we do remember them identifying Mary Magdalene as a prostitute and the woman who washed Jesus' feet at that diner. So maybe, we thought, our pastors don't always have all of the information available, or maybe we aren't getting all the information that is out there. Over the months following *The Da Vinci Code's* release, I watched as the novel dominated Google's list of top searches and Technorati's list of top blogging topics, and even before the perfectly crafted sermon series had been designed on PowerPoint, Christians were researching outside of their churches.

Most of us found out that Dan Brown sucks as a historical scholar of the New Testament and early Christianity. I mean who would mistake the Dead Sea Scrolls for the Nag Hammadi Library? (Insert nerdy snort here.) Nevertheless, we started reading about religion and Christianity online, and we learned things—like Mary Magdalene was never said to be a prostitute (which blew away my inspirational musical based about her life called "Whore Money") and that there were different forms of Christianity in the first and second centuries. But mostly we learned that there are volumes of information easily accessible online, and there are blogs and online communities where we can discuss all of this information. It was even slightly exciting to read this online information. In earlier centuries, a conversation about such topics would have been seen as heretical; you just didn't talk about things unsanctioned by the church. Well now you do; you blog about them, and anyone on the planet with an Internet connection can interact with you on the subject.

This accessibility is of great importance to contemporary Christianity, as it is changing the way we interact with information about our faith. We have access to more information about the New Testament and early Christianity than any other decade since that of Jesus. That changes the landscape for the contemporary church. We have unlimited amounts of information available at the click of a mouse, and this is likely a first for the religious communities as a whole. The laity has access to most of the information that the clergy have access to. And though we haven't been trained in the discipline, we have the same tools available.

RESISTANCE IS FUTILE (UNLESS YOU HAVE DIAL-UP)

I am not saying that every churchgoer has read *The Da Vinci Code* and then all of them immediately ran to the Internet. But there were a good bit who did, and while they were online, they were plugging in, not just consuming this information and leaving.

The technological revolution has connected info-maniacs together into social networks. This networking is becoming part and parcel to all major websites. That wasn't always the case. In the early days Bulletin Board Systems (BBS) facilitated chats that didn't take place in real time. It was like using the DOS operating system and only being able to access whatever the host was providing on his server. There were no graphics, and the system only took text-based commands. Generally an administrator would provide the majority of the content for people to log in and access, which was fairly limited. That changed as Internet speeds increased, web hosting became cheaper, and Internet Relay Chat (IRC) and AOL created chat rooms, instant messaging and the ability to host user content. Soon users were able to host their own websites easily. But the information was still created by a single user; other users had limited ability to interact.

Skip the long series of incremental developments and go right to the boom of MySpace, Blogger, Facebook and online forums. User-created content became king, and the host of a site only brought half of the equation; the interaction with and between users became the life-giving part of a site. Users could comment and link to and from information, they could vote on things, voice their opinions and meet people from all over the world. Blogging has created an easy and free Internet publishing domain, and all of these forums have generated huge, global conversations, with MySpace even showing us that communities can be formed and maintained completely online without so much as meeting a person face to face.

These networks have a couple things in common: They are mostly "open source" in that they are free and allow users to contribute to the content. They are setting a standard for new web platforms, in that the strongest way to have a web presence now is to have an interactive web presence that lets your users add to the content. And as they are setting this standard, they are creating relationships and connections that would have never existed before (much like how we are traveling more but this time it is online).

Open source is a term that is used in the software world to refer to an application that is available for free, along with its source code, or its program code, so that the users can modify the application and change it to make it better or more useful for them. Some software engineers say that open-source software has changed application programming as we know it. Many programmers are finding that they can create better applications when they let the users toy with them in order to see what additions the users actually want. This has also proven to be a free way to test your software.

For my purposes, I will use "open source" in the Wikipedia sense of the word: I use it to describe any presentation or organization that isn't top-down but is created organically from a number of sources that contribute something to the whole. This idea may change our theology in the same way that physical traveling does.

Interacting with people who are unlike us will change us—not always in big and immediate ways but simply by the fact that when we hear more stories, we widen our perspective, and when we widen our perspective, we change—even if only slightly. I would argue that this change of perspective happens in our online communities, as we are blogging and adding friends and talking to people.

My first big perspective change occurred when I was traveling in

Australia, and it happened in a split second. I was home from a day of picking grapes and sat down to watch the evening news. I was staring at the screen and it just looked odd. I couldn't figure it out. The talking heads looked just like the Americans, but something was off—and it wasn't the iconic Aussie accent. Then it struck me: the map behind the news anchors wasn't centered on the United States or neutrally on the center of the globe, it was centered on Australia. This was the first time that I saw a representation that showed that my country was not the center of the world. From then on, I haven't been able to look at a globe with the immediate reference of the United States as the center of it all. I remember European, Australian and New Zealand maps as backgrounds.

I believe that the same thing is happening in these online social networks. In an online network I learned that over 95 percent of scientists believe that the earth is billions of years old.* From my churches and Christian schooling I was led to think that it was more of a fifty-fifty thing. Furthermore, through an online book discussion, I processed the fact that the story of Jesus saving the woman caught in adultery from a stoning was never in any of the earliest copies of the Gospels. It strikes me that it was online, not in a Sunday school class, where I worked through these things; it was on blogs and theology forums where I talked about the ramifications of these findings. This is probably because honesty and transparency aren't as dangerous online; maybe that's why all of us youth workers were flocking to The Ooze (http://theooze.com) to talk about theology ten years ago, because we could say things online that we couldn't say in church.

Sometimes I think the church gets scared of too many voices. When I was working with a church a couple years ago, I suggested an online

---

*Larry Witham, "Many Scientists See God's Hand in Evolution," *Reports of the National Center for Science Education* 17, no. 6 (November-December 1997): 33 <http://ncseweb.org/rncse/17/6/many-scientists-see-gods-hand-evolution>. See also Wikipedia, s.v. "level of support for evolution" <http://en.wikipedia.org/wiki/Level_of_support_for_evolution>.

forum for the people to connect and talk about various issues and topics. The overall concern was that "anyone could come on and say anything," and while this is a valid concern, it was my exact reason for wanting to make an online community for the ministry. That's the thing, isn't it? With this online revolution, there is an uncomfortable egalitarianism. You cannot control whether someone will read or write pro or con material on controversial topics like *The Da Vinci Code.* The clergy can't bring you the final word on online matters; you wade through that on your own at home.

I think that this is generally a good thing, because I believe we are all able to wade through information and find truth. I think that this can be done, and in fact works best, inside community, but I also think that a church building is too small a place to be a repository of all things that we believe to be true. I believe that the more voices we have, the better our perspective will be in the end—even if some of those voices are different than ours or say what we may consider to be wrong. It's important to have multiple voices, not only so that other perspectives may be considered and other concerns can be raised about discussion topics, but also so that the people involved know that their voices are important.

I would love to see the church approach its theology and methodology the same way students research academic papers. They take a number of sources, and get as many perspectives as possible in order to form their own theses—even reading voices that will ultimately disagree with the theses they form—and they develop a rounded-out voice to support their ideas. But instead of creating a paper to be read to a congregation, this metaphorical paper would be presented and discussed among the congregation as a community, like you would present a paper to colleagues. The point of this discussion and presentation is to provide a more involved and coherent community. The discussion does not presume uniformity, but creates space for questions to be given to the presenter.

I think the church should embrace the fact that it may not contain all there is to know spiritually. This is, of course, not to say that the church does not contain valid spiritual knowledge, but to think that a single institution holds all spiritual knowledge could be dangerous—and even the spiritual knowledge that it does hold should be open sourced and worked out within the community. The bit of the church that I am skeptical of are the parts that have not acknowledged the implications of a technological revolution—there may be truth "in here," but there are at least serious, viable assertions of truth "out there" that merit further inquiry. I think these churches would do well to become like most online communities, developing the habit of engaging a variety of voices, rather than anointing and consequently consuming one—that of the senior pastor. I have been a part of a church service that had three speakers who collaborated on the message and divided their time at the pulpit. I have been to another church that had a day of the week where anyone was invited to come and work through what the service or sermon would look like on the following Sunday. The members of the church staff gathered in the sanctuary and gave an outline of what the sermon series would be about for the next few weeks and what sort of plans the staff had. The pastor would describe what Bible verses he was planning, the music director would share what songs he was planning on using, and then anyone there could suggest Scriptures, stories, testimonies or song suggestions to add.

Churches can take a cue from bloggers in this way. The blogger is similar to the pastor in that he or she has the main guiding voice of the online space.[*] The blogger will create the original post, and then the online community of readers will respond. Often, the conversations that happen in the comments section of a blog become richer (and often longer) than the initial blog entry itself. The people who comment are

---

[*] I am not arguing that having a single, guiding voice is a bad thing. I think facilitators are an important role, but facilitators should try to include as many outside voices as possible.

typically committed to the blog, and the blogger genuinely respects their opinions. This is an example of an "open source" community.

Dave Andrews is the facilitator of a group called The Waiters Union in Brisbane, Australia, and I had the chance to spend some time with him and visit some of the events he hosted while I lived in Australia. I will describe The Waiters Union more later, but for now, I want to show what a physical community would look when the "comments section" is given room to grow larger than the blogger's "original entry."

One Sunday night, Dave was driving me home from a church service he organized. Now most of the people who attend his services are societal outcasts and many have a mental disorder of some kind, but they are all invited to participate, even serving Communion. At the end of the night there is community prayer; anyone who wants to is invited to pray, and the congregation will respond and affirm his or her prayer by saying "Lord, hear our prayer." During the drive home, I remarked to Dave that we were asking the Lord to hear all those prayers, some of which were unintelligible and in some of which people asked for others to "get what they deserved." The latter was a little unsettling, but Dave explained that the importance of the prayer time in their community was not that we were all agreeing with what the people might have been asking for but that we are acknowledging the pray-ers' worth and their right, which exists just as much as mine, to pray to the Lord as they see fit—swear words and all.

I think we can learn a lot from Dave and the new infrastructure of the Internet. The age of technianity is here, where Christianity has come to face the technological revolution. The question is: How will I plug in? Others are already plugged in to things like The Ooze, which has been around for ten years and is a portal to get people and ideas together. Every couple of years The Ooze throws a learning party for those who are involved in order to develop community. At one of The Ooze's gatherings, Soularize, I met a handful of people in person who I had previously only known online, and during this learning party, I got to know them and they helped me develop my own ideas on theology.

Theologian Andrew Perriman's community, Open Source Theology (http://opensourcetheology.net), is an online forum for people to wrestle with huge theological topics, and there were some incredible discussions there after Perriman released his book *The Coming of the Son of Man.* This book explored how much of the second-coming activity expressed in the Bible has already happened: the great persecution, Jesus' spirit (or the Holy Spirit) having come upon the clouds already. This topic is seldom talked about in mainstream circles, but it exploded into a very deep discussion online. And though there is the occasional book bashing and slander, the majority of the website is filled with deep theological discussions. (It seems that the overall community weeds out those who don't want to contribute in a positive way.)

More mainstream, but just as potent, is Belief.net, where there are articles and discussions every day about theology. And as every child seems to now be infused with the ability to navigate through massive amounts of information with a few quick clicks, we are going to start seeing people in our churches come with new questions from conversations that they are having with their other church, their online church—or maybe they won't be going to a building at all, instead listening to a podcast from a couch and interacting with other listeners in the comments. That is technianity.

The Internet has created new social environments and new ways of getting information, and in some ways I think they go counter to the structure of traditional churches. When I realized how many perspectives I could get from the web, and the amount of information I could get easily, I started realizing how many viewpoints I wasn't getting at my church. My social network at my church was extremely small, and we all thought very similarly. This made me think that maybe the way my church (and probably many churches) processed information didn't foster growth so much as it cultivated conformity—not maliciously or even wittingly, but steadily and even unavoidably. It has led me to a deeper skepticism of church structure—all because new forms of relating to people and gathering information and learning about truth have opened up to me.

This skepticism is most pronounced in me when I look at how we construct our Sundays with the typical worship program. The way things are currently laid out don't seem to click with the way I see people processing information, or even community. So I am most rattled about the larger institutional structure and programming. I don't think that we need to throw the institution out, but I think that the structure needs a tweak—perhaps to look more like an open discussion.

OPEN-SOURCE SUNDAYS

I have always wanted to be one of those hard-hitting journalists who has a story that brings down some huge evil corporation. I admire those kind of journalists' reckless pitbull tenacity that leads them to break stories of corruption and scandal to the general public. Growing up in the age of corporate Enrons, I used to think that all institutions were evil, and if the church was an institution, then it was equally guilty of evil. But the truth is that, on the whole, churches—Protestants, Catholics, the Eastern Orthodox—aren't hotbeds of illicit, evil activity, and if I wanted a story that would encompass all of them (like they are conspiring to hide some big truth), I wouldn't find it.

That being said, from time to time there are some awful stories about churches in the news that make us all sick: married ministers sleeping with people in their congregations, clergy abusing children and money scandals, but these stories really are the exception to the rule. Of course, the exception always gets the most news coverage. However, with the number of religious institutions that exist around the world, the chances that your overseer is doing something absolutely evil is statistically very low, and the chances that he or she is giving up way too much of time to help the people around them is very high.

So it is not the recent news stories that make me skeptical of the institutional church. Rather, it is primarily the boom of technianity and the new ways that we've been able to collectively think through things in public forums online. I have been exposed to communities that are not structured in the ways that most churches are structured, and I have seen a model work that some church leaders have blatantly told me is "unbiblical and would not work." Churches as a whole (and forgive me for the overall generalizations) work in a very top-down manner; the pastor is the head of the congregation and is in charge of the worship experience and the presentation of the message on any given Sunday, Wednesday or, sometimes, Friday. Depending on the denomination, above the pastor there is some kind of governing body for the diocese, presbytery or district; this governing body establishes doctrine for the denomination and keeps an eye on churches' finances and ordinations (among some of the many other things that these governing bodies do). Many of us pick a church based solely on the church's denomination, and we do this because we know the doctrinal roots of that denomination, thus we know that this particular church's doctrine will be kept in sync by the governing body with the other churches under the same umbrella.*

So the service that you have on Sunday is a compilation of the denominational stance of the church, the pastor's thoughts and the community's style of music and presentation of the sermon and order of worship. The part of this structure that I am skeptical about is that the Sunday morning sermon and its central perspective is typically from a single person or a single viewpoint. The elders may take the preacher to

---

*Again, I want to emphasize that I don't think that anyone is power hungry or trying to have a monopoly on the church, so for the sake of argument, let's just assume that everything here is on the up and up. This is just a common church structure—though Catholic or other high-church denominations, like Anglicans or Presbyterians—are structured even more tightly, but I will use this common and general structure.

task if they feel that he or she has overstepped the bounds, but presumably all the elders and the minister are from the same doctrinal camp.

If you disagree with the pastor, you will generally reserve those thoughts for a private chat with him or her, for a Sunday school discussion or for a talk over a Sunday lunch at the buffet restaurant that your congregation frequents, but the content of the sermon is not open source. You are not provided with the content before the sermon; rather, you are presented a view of Scripture and left with that. Again, this isn't an evil corporation that is holding the secret of Jesus' marriage under the narthex somewhere; this is just the structure that the church has taken on over its long life.

Protestants, such as my stock, could say that we inherited this structure from the Roman Catholics. Or we could say that because many of the early Christians were uneducated and couldn't read, they needed to be given scriptural views because otherwise they'd be unable to form their own. In fact, Sunday school was said to have been started so that uneducated poor urban children could get proper schooling on their one day away from work before attending the Sunday church service. So I wouldn't argue that this structure came from a power play to control the congregation. I think that this single-voice structure was formed by a steady evolution, and by and large the congregational community never had too much against the idea.

I question this structure now because that is not how we form community anymore. We don't have only one news channel or a solitary book on U.S. history or a single authority on any work of literature. So if we wanted to discuss literature, there is no way that we would only use once source, even if that one source was the long-standing, authoritative text on the subject. We have varied accounts of the information on any topic, and there is often a book that will refute the work of almost any other book on the topics of theology, history, art or politics. Theological and biblical literature is so robust that it cannot be contained by a single person's perspective; this is evidenced by the fact that we keep producing different volumes of commentaries and opinions about the Bible.

However, while most of the pastors that I talk to agree with that point, they also believe that there is no way to incorporate the knowledge various scholars, as well as the accepted knowledge of the faith community, that would not lead to chaos on a Sunday morning. Even though they might be right, I disagree and believe it is possible. I believe that we have to have a bit of hope in people, and trust that if we believe in people and give them a chance to share their thoughts, we won't run our communities into chaos. Plus, I think that we need to be a bit skeptical any time we only have one voice talking.

Doug Pagitt, a leading voice in the emergent conversation, seems to have found some great ways to incorporate many voices into the services in his community, Solomon's Porch, which he used to stream at the community's website (www.solomonsporch.com). Besides the church's trendy music, lighting and artistic expressions, Doug provides the text on the church's large projector screen to every note that he is going to speak about, and he shows the whole chunks of the Bible that he will be reading from, not just a single verse. He also has a time following the message for the community to process the information together, where anyone is free to give his or her thoughts. Solomon's Porch is intentional about including members in every aspect of the service, as well as in the giving of the message itself.

I'm not trying to prescribe a way to do this in everyone's congregation, I just want to highlight why I am a little skeptical of the current structure and show that there are people who are changing the traditional ways of Sunday. Incorporating more voices into our services will vary based on particular communities, but there is precedent in Scripture and in the early church for a multitude of people to add their voices to a church's gathering. I think it would be worth looking into what we can do to make our own congregations multivoiced.

The first place your imagination may run when I discuss the idea of an open-source Sunday morning is that a debate or an argument will erupt, or worse yet, that some crazy person will proclaim that Jesus is coming on a comet so we best buy some track suits and plan a mass suicide. While I guess that this is possible, I don't think that it will take an open-source Sunday to have this happen. The scariest cult activity comes not out of an open-source Sunday where the platform is open for anyone to share ideas, but when there is a single leader holding all the authority. For every example of insanity that might happen if we open up the platform on Sunday mornings, I can give another example of where a single leader has led a whole group way off base. Because people aren't perfect, if unchecked, even community leaders can be led into great temptation.

GOOGLE IT

Many organizations are taking on this open-source structure and giving employees more responsibility to come up with bottom-up solutions and also giving them room to speak their suggestions. Google is one of the companies that is doing this best. It has been named as one of the top companies in the world to work for. In addition to completely taking care of their employees with healthy lunches, great health care, plenty of time off and childcare, they also give their employees a great environment to work in and ample time for their own pet projects. These projects aren't what they are being assigned to do during their normal day; they are getting paid to do whatever they want and create new applications of their own choosing, which they list on www .googlelabs.com. Google is an innovator in its field, largely because it gives the tools for all of its employees to contribute to the big picture. This wouldn't translate directly into an open-source Sunday, but it shows how this concept works in the Fortune 500 business world, which could easily work in the church since the contemporary church is modeled pretty closely after modern business structures.

I am skeptical of the institution because I am generally skeptical of top-down leadership. I am skeptical when organizations don't feel comfortable when their lessons, sermons and even statements of faith become open sourced. I believe that a church should be a bastion of equality and an example of how a healthy community can value every member equally, and part of that means that it will have to find ways to show how it values each individual. Most contemporary faith communities are literate assemblies of people who have a great wealth of life experience, as well as some knowledge about what is being talked about on a Sunday morning. Why don't we trust each other to give a hand? Why do we have to relegate any outside opinions to a Sunday school class or an after-church discussion? The point of lending a hand wouldn't be to completely obliterate the role of the pastor, but to let the pastor work as an overseer who would help direct the community of voices forward, agreeing where they agree and challenging where they are different—but allowing these voices in. A pastor could become, in a large part, a facilitator of these multiple voices, whose main job is to bring his or her training and education to the community, but also find and amplify the voices in the community that have training and education. The pastor is still leading the community toward unity.

Having a single person bring a message every week raises two potential risks: having people go away in discord because they disagree but don't have a healthy way to voice it, or conversely a community of people who look and sound exactly like the leader (which would be fine if the leader was 100 percent correct about 100 percent of what he or she said). This way of leading makes possible a very narrow community that doesn't encourage everyone to participate and doesn't give the members a chance to learn how to work out theology for themselves. Rather, they get used to being presented with information from a single source and trusting it as given.

I am not, by any means, suggesting that we get rid of the role of a pastor or leader of a community. In the same way local communities need some sort of accountability, the community itself needs to have an overseer, and we should respect the specific training that a pastor has in the areas of Scripture, doctrine and leadership. However, I am suggesting that we shouldn't make a pope of a pastor, and we should allow Sunday mornings to become more conversational as we figure out how to incorporate the pastor's theological teaching into time that includes our insights and questions.

The overall challenges for communities to turn into open-source communities could be numerous. First, there is the simple fact that most people are accustomed to sitting down and facing forward on Sundays, so we aren't necessarily ready to have comments. In a similar way, most people are nervous about speaking up in a gathering. We aren't that comfortable giving our opinions on theological matters; when we have given our opinions in the past, it is been in private conversations or in a small group. While there are the occasional characters who love to be the center of attention, for the most part public speaking seems to make it on the top of phobia lists these days. Then there is the fact that people will say things that are neither correct nor constructive to the community at large.

I don't intend on telling you how to change your specific community into the type that is open sourced on Sundays. However, on your way to become open sourced, I can tell you what not to do: You don't become open sourced by finding someone's giftedness and relegating them to that area. For example, if someone is gifted with children, I don't think you ought to put him or her in the nursery every Sunday; that nursery worker's very thoughts on God should be allowed into the conversation of theology on Sunday. You also don't become open sourced by doling out tasks to different people on a Sunday morning, such as reading an assigned verse or giving a prayer. It's great to have members read and participate, but having someone do a planned task, in and of itself, does not create an open-source environment. An open-source environment is one that has complete inclusion at every level of operation, which levels the playing field in conversations between the leaders and the people in the pew.

However, I do know a few things: open-source Sundays are attainable, and there are people doing them now. It seems that in the early church, a lot of people would bring a lot of different aspects to the service (1 Corinthians 14:26). This seems to work, because conventional knowledge tells us that two heads are better than one, it seems best to put our heads together when working out things like eternal salvation and other doctrines that teach us how to live. Since many of us are traveling and having experiences that are teaching and changing us—even if it's only sitting down to dinner with the History Channel on in the background—it might be advantageous to develop communities that not only respect the education of our pastors but also use our own educations and specialties to facilitate a more robust conversation on a typical Sunday morning.

It's a great challenge, but I think, in light of the way that we are seeing new types of online communities structure themselves, it may be good to get ahead of the curve.

OPEN SOURCE IS FREE

My immodest proposal: I personally think (brace yourself; this is crazy) that all churches need to close their doors for the next five years.

Harsh, right?

Maybe, but if we carry the idea of "open source" into our communities, we should acknowledge that open-source software is free. I think that money ties into our idea for a church that is an open-sourced environment. But imagine this: a recent poll said that if all the evangelical Christians in America would give 10 percent of their income to the poor, then we would eliminate extreme global hunger immediately. So if churches closed their doors for five years and American evangelicals directed 10 percent of their income toward a solution to the global hunger problem, then extreme poverty would be eliminated. Maybe then we could put in place measures to guarantee that it would stay that way.

The problem is that we are *institutionalized*. The church has buildings. They use them for gatherings, and they also use them to help the community. But with the amount of debt and bills that the average church has to pay, they can't just close the doors—nor could all churches find ways to operate without a building unless they restructured.

So my proposal isn't an actual proposal, and I know it won't happen. However, it does provide an image of why I am skeptical about giving money to a building. I like to give money to causes, to people in need, but I have problems giving money to buildings. Understanding, of course, that all organizations have overhead, when I give I want to give to places that can make my money go the furthest.

There was a report done by the one of the guys over at Relational Tithe (http://relationaltithe.com) called "The Embezzlement Papers." In these papers, there is a startling statistic that says about 90 percent of a church's budget stays inside the church. From working in a church I understand where that money goes. The money disappears quickly through salaries, utilities, mortgages, resources, mailing stuff, Sunday-morning handouts and so on. In fact, it is similar to what happens in our own homes with our own paychecks; they disappear on the necessities before we have a chance to spend any of it on something other than living expenses. I am not saying the church is hoarding money, but I do have a hard time giving my money to help a building stay afloat when there are options to giving my money to places that can use more than 10 percent of it to help those less fortunate than I am. In fact, there are some groups that can use all or most of my contribution for purposes other than interior bills: groups like Blood Water Mission, which is setting up wells in Africa; Kiva, which makes microloans for impoverished people working to start a business; International Justice Mission, which hires lawyers for those who can't afford them; or Bread for Life and the One Campaign, which are working to eliminate hunger.

Maybe I have just heard too many sermons about being a good steward, but it seems to me like being a good steward of the money I have means that I should ensure that my money goes as far as it can. And, for whatever reason, my money can go farther with a group like Kiva than it can with my local church. It could be argued that a local church is doing something in its community that impacts the community to the same degree that giving money to an aspiring business-woman in a developing country does, but I am wary of this when I see the budget dollars going predominantly inward.

I don't want to get preachy about money or even suggest that we shouldn't tithe, but while traveling and meeting people who can make 10 percent of my income go a lot farther than paving a new parking lot, I find it hard to give to the church. Not that I don't believe in expanding a faith community, but when given the chance of financing a foreign child's education or helping out with a church's mortgage, having traveled to see the children of other countries has pushed my bias toward them.

CONCLUSION

I hope that open-source Sundays will become part and parcel of the modern-day church. I hope that the church will acknowledge and find ways to accommodate the vast amounts of online information resides and interaction that goes on outside its walls.[*] A lot of churches are overdue for an upgrade, but until that happens, I remain skeptical of the institution, yet hopeful because of places where I see the task being taken on.[†]

---

[*]There are places that are accomplishing this, and I will talk later about the specific places that are managing to address these concerns of mine—as well as the places that have found creative ways to bring the church into a society that is dominated by the fast-paced, open-sourced way of social networking.

[†]For further reading on why twentysomethings are leaving the church, check out "The Exodus Papers" <www.iamjoshbrown.com/blog/2006/09/09/the-exodus-papers> or "Letters from Leavers" <http://lettersfromleavers.com>.

6

Scripture

TACKLING THE SUBJECT OF SCRIPTURE isn't something that I take lightly.

I will admit that I am only an amateur student of biblical literature, and my formal training does not extend beyond some undergraduate courses and piles of secondhand books. So while I am not an expert on the breadth of early Christian writings as a whole, I still consider myself somewhat informed.

Because of the process of becoming informed through my formal and informal education, and while I was looking through my beliefs in the same way that I was looking through my possessions before I moved across the world, Scripture got lumped into the category of things I am skeptical of. And the mountains of books I had on Scripture had to go through a gauntlet of scrutiny as I decided what to keep. In the end, I kept about a dozen books on Scripture, but the ones that I kept were those that contained warnings—warning about falling into errors of interpretation or misunderstanding context or incorrect theologies or perhaps even warnings about possible changes to the Bible. These books on warnings became important to me because the Bible is one of the most influential books in history—if not the most influential—and whenever something reaches that status, I think we must take every caution to approach it with the sort of honest criticism that something of its magnitude deserves.

So even though Scripture sticks with me and I saved quite a bit about it physically, I still box most of it up in the "skeptical of" category.

IN THE BEGINNING

The last hundred years could quite possibly be the most exciting time to be alive—though people probably say that about every century. But what can I say? This is the one that I am captivated by. In addition to the number of theologians that have come to the forefront in the 1900s, there have been some exciting archaeological discoveries. In fact as I was writing this chapter, an archaeologist just discovered a small piece of pottery that contains the oldest Hebrew writing that we have yet to uncover. The piece is over three thousand years old and seems to have been written by a well-trained scribe; it dates back to the time of King David, and even though it is small, it could tell us a lot about the laws and codes being followed at that time. Like I said, it is an exciting time to be alive.

We could also say that the most important ancient, historical documents have been discovered in the last hundred years. Specifically the two major finds are the Dead Sea Scrolls and the Nag Hammadi texts.* Both of these collections were found in bizarre acts of coincidence involving desert men finding old jars. These poor, desert men used parts of these documents to start fires, or they lost parts of them, or they sold or were conned out of the rest of the pieces. The manuscripts then traveled the world, were dated and translated, and were held

---

*I will go ahead and admit that I am an archaeology nut. It may be that in the next few years I will go back to school to study archaeology and disappear in the field, but for now I just read bits and pieces from the local library. I dream that I am part Indiana Jones and part Lara Croft (of Tomb Raider fame), which would be like having a cool fedora hat, a whip and some short, black shorts.

away from the public for decades—though eventually, consumers would be able to pick up copies of these documents in bookstores everywhere.

The Dead Sea Scrolls have given us extraordinary insight into a group of ascetic Jewish apocalypticists in the two centuries before Jesus; they also contain some of the oldest copies of certain Old Testament writings. The Nag Hammadi texts have given us equally interesting insights into communities that existed between one and two centuries after Jesus. These documents provide a frame of reference for the life of Christ, with a community of Messianic Jewish zealots on the one end and an ascetic community that formed based on some of the teachings of Jesus, which they combined with some secret knowledge that they said would help them interpret Jesus' teachings, on the other. In the former community, we read about the people who first began expecting a coming Messianic figure, which would set the stage for Jesus.

Now, you may have absolutely no interest in these two discoveries, because these texts do not only contain copies of canonical Scripture, but I would argue that even if you don't believe that these noncanonical texts are God-breathed, they are still of the utmost importance in helping us understand Jesus' own life and times. And I can assuage your fears and let you know that they do not say that Jesus was married or that he had a child.

In addition to the amount of information these texts contain about communities before and after the life of Jesus, they also contain the oldest biblical text in the canon that has been found—a copy of Isaiah dating back to 100 B.C. This is exciting because the older the manuscripts we find, the closer to the original we possess. Personally, these discoveries and this history are important to me on a spiritual level, because that skeptical side of me needs to find out more about the books that we claim hold God's very words. In finding older manuscripts we find better translations of Scripture, and we find that we can trust a lot of what has already been translated.

The reason I'm contemplating Scripture, and trying to find which box my hopeful-skeptic mind can put it in, is not to cast a doubt on a version of Scripture based on the archaeological discoveries of the last hundred years. Rather, it is to embrace that we are still learning about Scripture. If you believe that the Word of God is living and active, you have to admit that it wasn't born in the form of the New International Version. We are still finding copies of the living Word buried alive in the desert, and scholars are still picking it apart. For the avid reader of church history, it is interesting to see these texts being given fresh life and perspective.

In some ways, Scripture itself is like us. It is changing—to the extent that we are learning more about it. As we travel back in time through manuscripts that are closer to the originals and we learn more about the Scriptures it slightly changes. For my purposes, I want to wrestle with the idea that Scripture is sometimes slippery when we try to grasp it too hard, by which I am referencing the translation, transformation and passing down of the whole, more than just the internal stories. However, I do want to bring up a story about a guy—or rather a girl.

A SCRIPTURAL SEX CHANGE AND TEXTUAL CRITICISM

Junia or Junias? Growing up I was infused with the belief that the Bible, while not only being holy as the name denotes, was also infallible. I was taught that the traditional understanding of the "inerrancy of Scripture" was that the Bible was void of error in its history, science or even translation. To me, the Bible was written by the very hand of God and was a glimpse of the perfection of the Lord, so in essence, we had one perfect thing on earth. I remember being told the stories of the scribes who would wash their hands after every chapter they finished and who would destroy a whole document if they made a single error.

Then I learned about textual criticism.

When I took religion classes in college, I received a whole new perspective on Scripture. The perspective was that "liberal" one that I was warned about in all of those Don't-Lose-Your-Faith-in-College tracts, which I got at graduation from the Bible teachers at my Christian school. As you might probably guess, in secular, scholarly institutions, the Bible is recognized as a human creation—though this does not preclude it from divine influence. However, since we cannot prove divine influence, we examine the text as a human text. An error is seen as an error. The teacher does not act as an apologist, trying to fix discrepancies, but rather the teacher points out logical possibilities as to why discrepancies would occur in a text.

When I went to college I still had the view that the Bible was perfect; God had protected it for centuries as people, who were just as inspired as the original authors, translated it. The major hit to that assumption was made by a lady with the name Junia. She is a biblical character with a small part, but she is mentioned by Paul in Romans 16:7. A lot of us recognize that women had significant roles not only with the ministry of Jesus but also in the spread of the gospel in the early church. It may be that a male-dominated leadership structure had buried this in the past, but with the exception of a few denominations that don't allow for women to lead in faith communities, the Christian church has reassessed the position of women based on their early roles of leadership.

Junia is one such woman. Paul referred to her and her cohort as apostles—the highest form of authority in the first-century church—and she remains the only woman who is addressed as an apostle in the Bible. I am enthused when I think that women held positions of leadership from the start of Christianity, but in my first New Testament class in college, I heard the story of Junia's sex change by scribes of the New Testament. Apparently some people who were working with the Scriptures, translating and copying them for us, may have decided that an apostle could not be a female, so they made the clever move of adding an "s" on the end of Junia's name when they were copying the texts. So Junia became Junias, a male name as determined by the new masculine suffix. This story caught me completely off guard, and it started to put our current canon into the "skeptical" box in my mind.

It is hard to know exactly what happened with Junia. The facts are that the oldest texts show that this was the female name Junia, but newer texts have the name Junias—a male name that doesn't show up in any other texts from this period, which suggests that it is not a male name at this time but a later construction. We can't say definitively that a scribe was trying to change Junia's gender—perhaps they just stunk at copying—but it does seem that the scribe(s) who copied this text changed the name because they would have either assumed that a woman could not be an apostle or wanted to change the fact that a woman was an apostle. The sad truth is that to this day our Bible translators still have the same problem. The most reliable translations accept the original Junia, but some of the more traditional translations still try to change Junia to Junias, and they think they get away with it by adding a footnote that says that the earliest manuscripts do, in fact, say Junia.*

This revelation didn't shatter my faith like it did to some of my Christian classmates who shouted "Anathema!" (not literally) at the inference that the Bible they had in their hands was not an absolute copy of the words of God. Rather, the effect that this story had on me was one that prompted exploration and a healthy dose of curiosity. I started reading scholars who took very seriously the changes that had been made to Scripture, scholars that believed it was possible with enough searching to find something very close to the original text of Scripture.

Textual criticism. There isn't a single biblical scholar in the world

---

*See Rena Pederson, *The Lost Apostle: Searching for the Truth About Junia* (San Francisco: Jossey-Bass, 2006); and Bart D. Ehrman, *Misquoting Jesus: The Story Behind Who Changed the Bible and Why* (New York: HarperCollins, 2005), p. 185.

who will say that the Bible you have on your shelf is the exact copy of what the original authors wrote. On one hand, we know that this would be impossible, because English was not used for writing any of Scripture. And even if the original autographs of Scripture were perfectly translated into English, there would be a small percentage of language that would get lost in translation—like the popular folk myth that Eskimos have as many words for snow as Bubba has for types of shrimp in *Forrest Gump.*

If you have ever taken a foreign language, you have realized that there are some words that just don't translate. If you ask your instructor about them, the instructor will reply that "the word doesn't translate, but it sort of means . . ." I am assuming that similar things happen when translating Greek and Hebrew. The amount of language lost in translation will probably never account for losing the intent of a story or the purpose of a letter, but we have to accept that we have lost a little bit of the language in our copies of Scripture, even if they were perfect copies, solely from the fact of translation.

When I learned that there was a little bit lost in translation, I picked up a copy of *The Key Word Bible,* so I could start tracing back the Greek and Hebrew to try to get a little closer to the original intention of a passage. Having a Bible that used Strong's numbers (which are numbers that are assigned to a list of Greek and Hebrew root words used in the Bible; certain Bibles use superscripted numbers so you can look up the original Greek or Hebrew root words) to give me the exact Greek and Hebrew words that were used gave me hope in the battle to find out exactly what the Bible said. But that hope was still sprinkled with the questions that came from stories like Junia's.

On top of that little percent of translation that might not carry over, I had to come to terms with the fact that not one of over five thousand fragments of scriptural texts that we currently have are the original texts. We don't have any texts that were written by the hands of the original authors; we have copies of copies of copies. But this didn't fracture my faith either. We don't have many originals of most ancient texts, and technically none of the books that we read today are hand-written, original copies either. They have all had spelling checks and edits and things changed, but those things don't necessarily change what the author intended. So while those edits may have clarified the author's original intent by using correct punctuation, we have to face that there have been changes nonetheless.

Studying textual criticism in college, I learned that Scripture has changed slightly during each copy. The vast majority of the changes amount to nothing more than spelling errors or grammatical problems, but on a handful of occasions, there is the change of a major word or the sex change discussed previously. Some of the discrepancies are very apparent; just read through the footnotes in your Bible and you will see all sorts of disclaimers that state "not in the original manuscript," or "earlier manuscripts say . . ." or "some manuscripts say . . ." (e.g., Matthew 18:11; 23:14; Mark 1:1; 15:28; 16:9-20; Luke 22:43-44; John 7:53—8:11; Acts 8:37; Romans 16:7, 24).

Textual criticism sifts through these differences in the texts we have and puts together better versions of our Scriptures. I find the school of textual criticism fascinating and have high hopes for its continued success. Some of the more optimistic scholars involved in textual criticism think that with enough effort we can get back to a more accurate copy of Scripture. And though some more traditional Christians see these scholars as eroding Scripture, some of the best translation work we currently have is from these same scholars who have spent their lives attempting to restore Scripture to the original, as much as we can with the resources we have.

Overall, these small errors that I've discussed don't deter me from seeing Scripture as a powerfully inspired set of books and letters, but they do allow me to separate from the idea that the book we hold in our hands is equivalent to the tablets that Moses brought down from the mountain. It has taken me twenty years, but I have come to grips with the fact that we don't have anything on earth written by the hand of God.

GOSPEL STORIES

Another turn of events for my college classmates and me was the professors' assertion that we may not have any eyewitness accounts of the life of Jesus that were written by the actual eyewitnesses. I had always thought that the authors of each of the four Gospels blogged daily on the life of Jesus, so I was flummoxed to find out that neither Mark nor Luke had ever met Jesus—though that fact had been in front of my face for my entire life.

It was as plain as day in the first four verses of Luke: the author was collecting the stories about Jesus from eyewitnesses, but he himself was not one. In addition, Luke says that he need to create an "orderly" account (Luke 1:3). We can only suppose that there was such a need because, at the time of the writing, there were (1) no accounts or (2) no orderly accounts. Mark, I would soon learn as well, was not a follower of Jesus but a follower of Peter, and he also got his information from someone else who was an eyewitness.

I don't know why we aren't always upfront that only two of our Gospels are attributed to eyewitnesses, but in my church experience this fact seems to be overlooked—just like sex and politics at the dinner table: never discussed. In addition to this fact, many scholars—like Bart D. Ehrman, Bishop John Shelby Spong, Ben Witherington III, Timothy Paul Jones and Bishop N. T. Wright—seem to agree that the Gospel writers used other sources for content, which Luke obviously admits to. It is further accepted that most Gospels started as collections of sayings, which had narratives built around them. For example, the *Gospel of Thomas* gives us an idea of what a gospel looked like to the early followers of Jesus, because this Gospel does not have any narratives and only contains quotes or sayings. More recently, Phyllis Tickle showed us what this might have looked like in her book *The Words of*

Jesus, where she stripped the Gospel narratives and only provided the words Jesus said.

If the Gospels did start out as collections of sayings, then I can't help but think that while the narratives were being fleshed out and while the original texts were being copied, some error may have entered into the accounts. Now, I'm not saying that these kinds of errors are ones that would omit a bride of Jesus, but maybe events are ordered out of place or told from a slightly faulty recollection. None of these things shatters my respect for or understanding of the Bible; it just makes me approach the biblical narratives with a healthy dose of skepticism, it makes me read those pesky footnotes and wonder why things weren't in the original, and it makes me cautious to accept any doctrine or worldview that is constructed by a single verse (e.g., snake handling = not in the oldest texts).

At the same time, while I battle with skepticism about the text and the problems some scholars have with authorship, I know that there are a number of hopeful scholars out there who believe that the stories are very accurate as they are. These hopeful scholars postulate that it would have been of utmost importance to preserve the stories of Jesus without error and with a good bit of corroboration and fact finding—like what Luke would have done.

Orderly accounts. I am a huge fan of the show *Lost* on ABC. In fact, I don't know if I have ever been such a fan of a network television show since *The X-Files.* Sometimes when I am traveling by plane, I wish it will, like the one in *Lost,* make an emergency landing on a Pacific island. But I will leave my escapist fantasies and move straight to a valuable lesson about Scripture that I learned from *Lost.*

One of the critiques made about Scripture is that the chronology is skewed in the different books of history and between the Gospel accounts. In fact, this was a major topic in one of my New Testament classes, as we tried to look at the Gospel accounts side by side, and it seemed that some authors could not have cared less about putting things in order. This led many professors to argue that individual authors of Scripture had specific reasons why they would order their accounts the way that they did and why they would tell stories differently than other authors, which sometimes created discrepancies between the Gospels. One professor even devoted two entire classes to the day that Jesus was crucified and the apparent discrepancy in the Gospel accounts. All of this discussion circled around timelines and why specific authors would want certain events on certain days. I had similar questions as I sat in my high school Bible class, reading the two creation accounts in Genesis. The first account has a creation order that differs slightly from the second account. In the first account, vegetation is made before humans, but in the second, it is the other way around. I couldn't wrap my head around why the accounts would be different, and so I was wary of viewing Scripture as literal, chronological and orderly.

Fast forward to a few years later: I am engrossed in the television-sensation *Lost*. Leslie and I prepare an hour before *Lost* to have snacks ready, mood lighting on and cell phones off as we salivate for the new episode to begin. One day, though, during this routine, I noticed something at the very beginning of the show; the announcer will say: "previously on *Lost*" and then give a recap while various scenes appear on the screen. The scenes are edited together to give the viewer a glimpse of what has transpired in the previous episodes or seasons, but the scenes are often out of order. They didn't unfold for the original viewer in the same way that they've been edited to catch up new viewers. And some of the scenes that appear aren't even in previous episodes; they're small clips that didn't make it into the actual episodes but were gathered from the cutting-room floor for the purpose of the recap. I started thinking about what the producers had done. They had skewed the order of events in order to make a small clip that would fill the viewers in on the major things the viewers missed. The producers hadn't really changed anything; they just recapped the events in a way that the story would make more sense to viewers and allow them to get up to speed as quickly as possible, while, at the same time, staying true to the story from the previous episode.

I wonder how many of our problems with the details in the story-telling in Scripture are just part of the voice of the storyteller. Perhaps Jesus actually did go to this city before that city, but the Gospel writer mixed up the order. Maybe mixing up the order was to make a specific point, or maybe the Gospel writer was a storyteller first and a historian second, with his main goal being to get the point of the story across before anything else. Who knows? But I think the writers do a good job of getting the message across. In fact, my overall beef with Scripture isn't actually the writers—though I think we need to understand that the fingerprints of the writers are all over the text—my beef and overall skepticism may really have more to do with the readers.

TEXT, CONTEXT AND METEXT

I majored in literature and creative writing in college, and I learned that you couldn't break any rules in writing until you mastered those rules first. Any time I would read a poet or an author who did something out of line with a particular writing guideline—maybe it was a poet who broke the preordained structure of a sonnet, blank verse or haiku—I would ask my teacher how he or she got away with it. My teacher would say that it was because they had "poetic license." So I would ask my professors when I would get my license, and the typical response (from a multitude of professors) was after I was published. So with license firmly in hand, I am inventing words, which is the favorite pastime of many authors before me. But before I jump into using my license, I need to talk about context.

Aside from translation errors, misrepresentations of a story or *Lost*-esque timelines, there is one elemental obstacle to overcome with any text—scriptural or otherwise. Context. Context is the perspective, which we must have about any story or work, we need in order to understand what the work was intended to mean as it was written, whether it is a Wilfred Owen poem about war or the rehearsed, stand-up comedy of Lenny Bruce. Context is critical background, and just like any other piece of literature, each book in canonical Scripture has a specific context.

To understand the Gospels, you have to, for example, consider Roman life, the average lifestyles of those in the first century, the first-century understanding of Jewish texts, the rights of Jews in the Roman Empire, what Galilean pietism was, what the political landscape was during the time, what insurrection Barabbas was a part of that got him arrested, as well as many other pieces of information. And that's just a small bit; the Gospels were written over about three decades, but imagine the amount of contextual material for the whole Old Testament, which was written over hundreds of years.

Herein lies my greatest skepticism—not in the jots and tittles that got fudged over in the translation years—with the stuff that gets fudged over today with each one of us, myself included. It happens more often than not that when we misuse Scripture, it is not because something was lost in translation but because we were not adequately informed of a specific text's context. This is one of the biggest problems with our use of Scripture. When we read a text that smacks of defiance to the Babylonian or the Roman Empire, we can easily forget the original context that the text was written in, and we try to decipher its meaning for today without considering the background. This happens every Sunday. Some people are so engrossed in using the book of Revelation as a set of tarot cards, anticipating the coming World War III, they forget that the references made in Revelation were to a past audience about past times. Even if some of the events described there do occur, to some extent, in the future, that book was written to another context and not about current-day Iraq.

The possibility of making a contextual error is a good reason to be careful when reading any text that was written in a different time and place than our own. However, I think there is another culprit that is a close brother of misreading context, and that is "metext." Metext is what I call whatever we bring to a text; it is our transposed personal context. Metext is that semidangerous ground that we enter when we graft ourselves onto the text. And it is, potentially, one of the greatest crimes in the literary world.*

Now, when we do it with more contemporary texts and experiences, it doesn't seem like that significant of a crime. It becomes kind of like jaywalking. Everyone jaywalks, and we might argue that jaywalking is often unavoidable because we lack adequate crosswalks. Metext is less of a distraction from authorial intent when I am reading a poem or essay that is current to my own time. For example, if I read a paper or a poem about terrorist attacks that happened in my lifetime, in my country, I will read them in light of my own feelings and understandings of the political landscape, and perhaps I might even think that the author was talking about things that I was feeling. And if the author is American and somewhat like me, then the metext may not be too far from the context, because the author and I are from the same time, talking about the same event and having similar feelings.

But what happens when I insert myself into a text that is over nineteen hundred years old? I can be assured my metext will not be comparable to the original context. This is where it gets sticky, because I agree with the theorists that say metext is unavoidable, but I think that when we substitute our metext for a valid and complete context, we tread in dangerous territory.

Without understanding the proper context, early American pastors used parts of Paul's writings to endorse slavery; they grafted their situations onto Paul's and assumed that when Paul made com-

---

*Many present-day literary theorists argue that metext is simply unavoidable. We can't approach anything, literary or nonliterary, as an empty slate. We bring ourselves to everything that we experience.

ments about slavery, he was not speaking to a certain group of people at a certain time but that he was making a universal endorsement that would last as long as people believed in the Bible. They were wrong. They didn't understand Paul's context. He was speaking to a specific situation, in a specific community, during a specific time. Paul's complete context must be the starting point, not our own understanding of the text based on reading a couple of verses in his letters.

Those of us growing up in a white, male-dominated, middle-class society will likely project a certain metext onto Scriptures that were largely written to ethnic minorities who lived in exile. For example, this metext might be driven by Americanism, colonialism, imperialism or consumerism, and we might make Scripture look more like a self-help book or a book on how to prosper financially. Someone caught up in the rat race of trying to achieve the American dream might flip through the Bible one morning and stumble across a guy named Jabez, who asked the Lord to increase his territory (1 Chronicles 4:9-10). Then, thinking that that prayer is about him and his American dream, he may read that passage as confirmation that his ambition to have more money is one that will be blessed by God. He might even start praying that prayer every day, believing more fervently that he should have more money and success. He may even go so far as to name his yacht *Jabez*, as someone in Chicago allegedly did, to remind himself that God wanted him to ask for prosperity. However, I can almost guarantee that an African pastor whose congregation has been wrecked by HIV/AIDS will read that prayer much differently.

So I get skeptical of how we treat Scripture. We often mix our own personal metext with our traditions' metexts, and then we mix those with the knowledge we have of the original context, as well as with some, maybe, ill-informed information about the context. All the while, what we really need to be doing is trying to understand the people to whom the author was writing, the situation the author was writing into or about, and what the author was saying to the people in that situation. Only when that is accomplished can we start to sift through if there are implications for us in the present. But we don't always do that; *I* don't always do that. That is why metext scares me. Certain metexts can turn obscure lines of Scripture into equations for how to get yachts.

Poetic devices. During a class trip that I went on to Jamaica, while I was taking a course on Bob Marley (don't ask), I had the privilege of attending an annual literary festival called Calabash. I got to meet one of my favorite poets, Cornelius Eady, and listen to him read his poetry. After his reading I met with him and talked to him about some of his poems. I told him that my class had been working with a poem of his called "The Supremes." He asked what the topic of conversation was in regard to the poem, and I told him that we were using gender analysis to entertain the idea that the main characters in the poem were cross-dressers. He started laughing and, in disbelief, said, "No, it is just about singing group The Supremes. Just like the title says." The metext there was the bias of gender studies, which had been applied to the poem, completely forsaking its glaring context.

Back to the boxes. Though I am hopeful that we can get Scripture pretty close to what it looked like as originally authored, I get skeptical because when we hold it in our hands, it becomes human. When I approach Scripture, I approach it as an ancient voice of wisdom that has been saved for me through and by the very lives of those who wrote and translated it. I take seriously the fact that I can physically hold a Bible; I know there is the blood of its faithful protectors on the printing presses. However, I also know that humans have a proclivity to project metext on everything—whether it is women's studies, African American studies, religious studies—and we very often put an incorrect lens up to something.

Could it be that we often miss the context? I believe we do many times when we read literature that is older than us, and for that reason, I think we need a healthy skepticism in how we read Scripture—not necessarily about the changes that may have occurred in the copying and translating but about the context that we may be missing.

7

Traditional Views of Jesus

I WAS DRIVING AROUND ATLANTA when I saw a familiar Christian bumper sticker; it read "Jesus is my copilot." Not more than thirty minutes later, a short amount of time in Atlanta traffic, I saw another car with a slightly different bumper sticker that read, "Jesus is my pilot." I was happy to see that, at some point, Jesus got a promotion, but at the same time I was equally concerned about Jesus' ability to fly a plane. I am pretty sure that Jesus could not fly a plane. If you time-warped him from the time period when he was on earth in bodily form straight to today, I don't think that he could.

Many people believe Jesus could do anything back then and could still do anything now if he were here in physical form, but we know that he was at least partially limited while on earth. We know that he had to eat and learn and grow, and many people believe he was not omnipresent or omnipotent while in human form. So I think it is fair to say that first-century Jesus could not fly a plane. I processed all of this while I spent the rest of my time in the car in the slow-moving Atlanta traffic. I get the point of the copilot or pilot metaphors, but this kind of bumper sticker leads me to the last of my major skepticisms: the thousand different faces of Jesus.

In general, bumper stickers are a bad way to talk about theology, because they aren't particularly conducive to discourse. They are made to be punch lines in the midst of a chaotic world that is flying past at speeds up to 100 miles per hour. In addition, they are breeding grounds for cheekiness and bad theology—a one-sided, hit-'em-quick way to throw beliefs out there and speed off. They are about as effective as yelling at people while flying by in a passing vehicle.

But I am as guilty as the next guy because my '87 Ford Taurus station wagon, The White Knight, had some great ones on it. Before I leave the idea of bumper sticker theology though, I have to address one of the most famous Jesus bumper stickers, the "My boss is a Jewish carpenter" one. This one is a piece of Christian Americana. I remember it from my early childhood: it was so simple, the blue background with the white text. I think about that one when I see bumper stickers every so often—especially when I think about all the different thoughts that we have about Jesus. For example, the idea that Jesus was a carpenter; there is only one Bible verse that mentions carpentry associated with Jesus, and while some versions indicate Jesus was the carpenter, others indicate his father was. In fact, we know quite little about his early life, and I can't find a single passage where it says that Jesus held a hammer or crafted wood. That doesn't mean that it is impossible that he was, but in our collective, unified thoughts, we seem to have decided that Jesus was a carpenter like his father.

When I sat in that New Testament class where I learned that some scribes had changed the gender of Junia, I also learned that Jesus' father, Joseph, was not necessarily even a carpenter. The Greek work that was used to describe Joseph is *ho tekton,* which simply means craftsman or artisan. This term does not preclude carpenters, but it doesn't specify the type of artisan. However, tradition has handed down the notion that Joseph was a carpenter and then we've inferred that Jesus must have been trained in the ways of his father—regardless of the fact that an angel told his mother that he would be God's chosen one and in spite of the fact that he received such magnificent gifts around the time of his birth that he probably would not have had to work a day in his life.

However, that carpenter bumper sticker doesn't bother me, because the truth is that it could be entirely accurate. Perhaps Jesus' father was a craftsman of wood, and perhaps Jesus worked in same trade as his father until he became an itinerate minister. My interest in this bumper sticker isn't because this particular tradition might be wrong, my interest is in how many of the simplest parts of Jesus' life, or all of Christianity for that matter, might be based on traditions or inferences that aren't ever explicitly stated in Scripture.

Because traditions and inferences can create many faces of Jesus, as readers of sacred Scripture we have the obligation to look at the text critically—without assumptions and without the metext—and to separate fact from tradition. Because of the kind of assumptions already described, the views of Jesus that we have adopted may be different than those of the early followers, and perhaps they may even miss some of the most important parts of Jesus' life.

This is the reason I am skeptical about traditional views of Jesus. If they are based purely in tradition, then I believe they are somewhat limited and perhaps misinformed. Perhaps each denomination relies on a specific picture of Jesus—maybe a fire-and-brimstone Jesus, a social–justice Jesus, a loving–friend Jesus, an anarchist Jesus, the options are endless—but I believe each of us has a Jesus that is very similar to the one described by the tradition that we were brought up in. But my objection isn't against any particular tradition's view of Jesus, it is against the notion that one tradition's picture can contain the robustness of Jesus or that any one tradition has the story 100 percent correct.

Taking apart prefabricated images of Jesus and stripping them down to be historically accurate could be classified under the large umbrella that scholarly types would call the search for the historical

Jesus. However, I don't think this search needs to be academic. Rather, if each community of faith were to understand that sometimes things that aren't necessarily in the text (like carpentry) get slipped into our stories about the nativity or the life and times of Jesus, we might be able to form an agreement to start with the fundamentals and work with the texts themselves in order to build a more accurate picture of Jesus. If we did that, I for one would be less skeptical of many traditions—if I could watch the face of Jesus be built up with denominational tradition *and* historical criticism *and* historical tradition *and* the community coming together to work through the various traditions and criticisms as a group. This isn't to say that we have to start at the beginning every Sunday, but if we make particular claims about Jesus, we should take the extra time to attribute where we get the basis for our claims.

Many people have tried to tackle this project of knowing and understanding the historical Jesus, and as easy it is to start with texts that can be laid as a bedrock and then build on them, we also need a good deal of cultural context. In the academic world, there are some great scholars who have spent their entire careers establishing a foundation on which to build a solid understanding of Jesus. Joel Carmichael wrote in his book *The Birth of Christianity* that the whole movement toward the kingdom of God has to be understood by starting with the idea that Jesus was crucified for sedition.[*] Hugh Schonfield, a British biblical scholar, said in his controversial bestseller *The Passover Plot* that "the fundamental teaching of Christianity, then, was that in Jesus, the Messiah (the Christ) had come. There can be not the shadow of a doubt about this."[†]

Recognizing that in Jesus, for Christians, the Messiah has come and also recognizing that, to some historians, Jesus was killed for sedition are two great ways to build a first-century sketch of Jesus and Christi-

---

[*]Joel Carmichael, *The Birth of Christianity* (New York: Dorset Press, 1992), pp. 207-9.
[†]Hugh Schonfield, *The Passover Plot* (Dorset, U.K.: Element Books, 1993), p. 19.

anity. While I am neither educated enough to talk at length about what people living in first-century Palestine were expecting in a Messiah, nor am I a historian who can eloquently write about the possible social effects that Jesus must have had on the Roman military state in order to be perceived as a political threat, I know enough to believe that there is no reason that we shouldn't be putting Jesus in those first-century contexts on Sunday mornings.

I have visited roughly 150 churches in the last twenty-five years, and I have only heard this type of contextual background a handful of times when trying to put a particular text in its cultural context. Now I can't say that my paltry 150 churches are any sort of sample of the church at large, and I know for a fact that there are churches that focus predominantly on first-century context any time that they speak of Jesus, but there are many that don't. This isn't necessarily the fault of pastors; certain teaching styles and certain denominational traditions don't lend themselves to including historical backdrops, but that brings me to my overall question: Is it possible that our churches sometimes have a limited tradition to draw on when it comes to discussing the scope of the life of Jesus?

THE PASSION

When Mel Gibson directed (and starred in—if you count the cameo of his hand holding one of the nails that held Jesus to the cross) the box office hit *The Passion of the Christ,* Christians came out in droves. Many churches changed into box offices and started hosting nights at the movies. And the movie had great success. I remember going to see it with a group from a church I was working with at the time, and it was, indeed, an experience.

If you haven't seen it, I am sure that you can piece together an idea of it if you think of the scene in *Braveheart* where William Wallace is cruelly tortured—then stretch that scene out into a whole film and insert Jesus. The content of the film was basically two hours of crucifixion. I remember one student walked out ten minutes into the cruci-fixion, and in the lobby afterward others were talking about how they couldn't wait for it to come out on DVD. I never purchased the film, and I don't ever plan on watching it again. It wasn't that the acting or directing was awful, or even that it was too gory for me (I happen to be a big Quentin Tarantino fan), but the film only focused on one event: the crucifixion. There was a split second of resurrection, but it was really only about the death of Jesus.

I understand that the point of the film was dramatic effect, but I think that something happened in this film that happens in many tra-ditions: we focus so much on Jesus' death that we miss some of the greatest parts of his life. Surely the death and resurrection of Jesus is enormously important to the Christian faith, but when it becomes the *only* focus, we miss his teaching and trade his words for his death. We forget that the red words of the New Testament are just as important as the red, blood-stained cross.

In the same way that faith without the death and resurrection of Jesus is incomplete, so is faith that is fixated only on his death and gives little thought to his life and words. I think Mel Gibson showed that many Christians' thoughts about Jesus don't go past that one act; that one act is the only Jesus tradition we carry. So *The Passion of the Christ* shows us what a single perspective on the life of Jesus would look like. Now Gibson, as an artist, has every right to take a single point in a life and stretch it into a full-length film; that's what directors do. And it can work in art, but it is problematic for theology.

The problem can surface where we take a single picture, story or event and stretch it to fit our entire theology. If our theology of Jesus is limited to his death, then we have the possibility of missing out on some of his words of life. Just like Gibson's film is fine in capturing those last days, it isn't helpful for telling me about Jesus' teachings. If I were to use that film to form a complete theology on Jesus (and that was not the purpose of the film) I would come up a little short. Although sometimes we do this in theology: sometimes we only see in the face of Jesus the face of someone who came to die.

THE LAST TEMPTATION

I don't have a problem with artistic renditions of actual events. So if we are going to speak of Jesus as a carpenter, I just wish that we would preface that statement with a disclaimer, "If Joseph was a carpenter, we can assume, then, that Jesus would have trained in the same vocation." This may seem like an unnecessary inconvenience, but in the end isn't it better to announce when you are speculating than to introduce people to a speculative Jesus?

When I watched *The Last Temptation of Christ* for the first time, I was all alone and had the door locked so that no one would know that I was intrigued by the film that had caused so much controversy. Now, many years since that viewing, the first thing I remember about the film is a disclaimer at the beginning of it, which announced that it was not based on the historical Jesus but rather on a fictional novel. I wondered why Christians would create such a fuss when the movie starts out with that sort of information. It admitted that it is a work of fiction. I only wish we would do the same when we make speculative stories in order to drive home a point during a talk or sermon.

However, there is one scene in the movie that has stuck with me more than any other, a speculative interpretation of a documented event. It was a heartbreaking scene and, to my surprise, a very similar event was recorded in the Gospels: Jesus' mother and family tried to meet him while he was on the road preaching, but Jesus looked at her, as the family was trying to get him to come home, and said that he has no mother or brothers—that his brothers and sisters are any of the children of God (Mark 3:31-35).

The film, even though largely fictional, showed how this conversation could have happened. It could have been a hurtful phrase for Jesus' mother to hear, and it could have been very callous. Certainly we don't know what Jesus' tone was, but the movie portrayed a speculative picture of a text. It gave us an idea of how the text might have been played out—but it didn't claim to be the so-called gospel truth.

Using art forms, the writer and director of the film painted a picture of what a scene might have looked like, and they left us with that to ruminate on—with their assumption being that their interpretation is only one way to read the event. Pastors often do the exact same thing, but sometimes they don't inform us that their thoughts are only one possibility or one side of Jesus' face. In fact, many if not most people don't preface their views of Jesus with disclaimers, so I get skeptical about those communities who think they have found the exact face of Jesus. They think they have him figured out. They speak of him like they would a spouse of fifty years, knowing every idiosyncrasy. But they don't. They may know a lot about Jesus, but they haven't had a perfect look, there is always something more to learn, and there is the chance that they have missed a thing or two.

So I will always be skeptical of any institution or particular tradition that limits Jesus as someone who has been completely figured out. And I will be further skeptical of people who keep him as a Jewish carpenter, but I become hopeful when that bumper-sticker slogan is turned on its ear by a bestselling book like *More Than a Carpenter.*

When people are able to see that their own perspectives or traditions aren't the only view, they are more open to presenting images of Jesus from other vantage points, which can allow the first-century Jesus to explode into the multifaceted personality that he is—a personality that is not confined by tradition but divinely transcends any one image of him. Some churches and faith communities are excellent at pulling this off. I have been to gatherings that allow speculation and alternatives to the single-view reading of Jesus' words, and I have seen this done in a way that doesn't create new traditions that we stick to the image of Jesus. Rather these new perspectives, this speculation, can actually deepen our understanding by helping us separate our preconceived ideas from the actual person of Jesus. The right environment can free us to distance ourselves enough from our tradition that we can explore alternatives we have missed altogether.

Pete Rollins describes a certain gathering of Ikon, his community in Northern Ireland, in his book *How (Not) To Speak of God.* At this gathering, each member of the group was given a picture of Jesus, and at the end of the night they dropped the pictures they were holding into a fire, showing that no one picture can capture the complete Jesus. In fact, many times we hold icons that are representations of Jesus or God, but they are in themselves only idols.

8

Civil (Dis)Obedience and Revolutionary Change

I THINK A HOPEFUL SKEPTIC IS ALWAYS on the move, moving from a position of ongoing questioning and skepticism to a position where they will get fed by hope and will be led to action. I believe hopeful skepticism is necessary for the institutional church, and I think there is room to have creative hopeful skepticism break into situations and slightly alter the ethos of a worship service or even an entire community—maybe then the community will become a better place for hopeful skeptics to find a way to faithfully follow Jesus with a questioning mind.

Below are a few responses of hopeful skeptics to those inside of and outside of the church. One story is even about a hopefully skeptical leader who decided to change the whole structure of his community because of his skepticism about the current structure. However, please keep in mind that none of my stories are prescriptive; I am not writing a John Maxwell–type book that contains "The Twenty-One Indispensable Codes for Becoming a Great Hopeful Skeptic." Rather, I just want to provide concrete examples of how the hopeful skeptic can enrich spiritual relationships and communities—because, for all my skepticism, I am very hopeful.

OTHERS ARE SKEPTICAL OF US, WHY NOT BE SKEPTICAL OF OURSELVES?

I finished up my bachelor's degree studying English at Georgia State University in Atlanta. When I transferred there I decided that I immediately liked the college, because unlike my previous college (the University of Alabama), it wasn't a small southern town with good ole boys (though there were plenty of them, but they didn't define the campus). Georgia State was diverse, as diverse as the streets of downtown Atlanta that wove through it, and while I was there, I met all kinds of people who helped round out some traditional, narrow, southern Christian views I had.

One of my favorite experiences was a lunch I had in 2004 with a newfound friend on campus. Jeffim was European, had grown up in three countries, knew four languages and was attending Georgia State. I don't remember how we ended up eating lunch together one afternoon, but we sat in one of the many café-style restaurants downtown and shared a vegetarian meal between classes.*

Jeffim and I sat and ate together for an hour. We talked about Europe, his travels, the attacks of September 11, George Bush, indie music and other collegiate topics. But then he asked me why I moved to Georgia. I cringed.

I didn't want to talk about church. I hated talking about working in a church to people who were outside the church. I wasn't embarrassed

---

*As a bit of background, I should mention that I had come to Georgia to be part of an internship in a large United Methodist Church just outside the perimeter of Atlanta. It bothered me that I moved solely for the internship, because that meant that every time someone asked me why I moved to Georgia, I would have to talk about church. Hip church workers like me usually hate that (except for the overly zealous ones who want you to come to their church and will recount stories of the conversations they've had on planes, where they shared the Romans road with the passenger next to them—those people *love* to be asked what they do; they live for it).

about the job, but it immediately separated me from the rest of the world. It makes an "us and them" feeling drape over any two conversationalists. Reluctantly, I told him about the internship anyway, and when I did, his whole appearance changed. He said quickly, "Oh God, you aren't one of those [expletive] Christians are you?"

That was the single worst response I had ever received from anyone when I've said that I work for a church. Even in my craziest hallucinations, I couldn't imagine such a response. *Was I what he thought I was? What did he think I was? Could I be as awful as he thought I must be?*

I decided I couldn't be. I mean, I had as many questions about Christianity as he probably did. Whatever he associated Christianity with, I know I wasn't part of that: I didn't proselytize, I was concerned about the environment, I was embarrassed about the Christian history of violence, I was ashamed of the Bush administration—just like him. No, I was not what he thought, but how could I convince him?

What I said next may have been the best answer I could come up with at that particular moment, summing up my feelings with types of Christians that I had just been lumped in with. Swallowing my tofu, I said, "Yeah, but not like any of the [expletive] Christians you must have encountered."

That was most likely the comment that solidified our friendship, and from then on, we talked many more times about spirituality. For that moment, in that context, what I had said was the perfect answer because it acknowledged the fact that I was hopeful about following Jesus (yes, I am a Christian) but dubious about traditional and institutional forms of Christianity (but not like any of the [expletive] Christians you must have encountered).

A hopeful skeptic will talk differently than other Christians about the things they value. We must carefully hold two worlds—the world that we want and the world that we question—and we share in the questions others have about our own faith.

HISTORICAL HOPEFUL SKEPTICS

During the time that my wife, Leslie, and I spent in Australia, we found ourselves in Brisbane, where we met up with Dave Andrews (who I mentioned in chap. 5). Dave is a person who is hard to capture. I could describe him physically, or I could call him an activist, or I could define him by his work as an author or as the originator of the Waiters Union or as a musician, but none of those would completely encapsulate him or the work he does.

Dave and his wife, Angie, invited Leslie and me out for dinner when I told him that we were in Brisbane, and we ended up getting to spend a good bit of time with them during the two months we lived there. However, one night after dinner at Dave's house, we shared some tea and I found out a little bit more about Dave and the heart of the Waiters Union. I had hoped to interview Dave that night for the podcast, but instead we just talked without any particular agenda, as he shuffled through some books and taught me about Christian revolutionaries.

I learned about people like Clarence Jordan, who started an interracial farming community in the American South during the heated times of the civil rights movement; Jim Dowling and Ann Rampa, political activists who are members of the Catholic Worker movement and anti-war movement in Australia; and Toyohiko Kagawa, a peace advocate and Christian reformer from Japan who worked for economic reform, women's suffrage and workers rights. These revolutionaries are people who believe that the way of Jesus is a revolutionary lifestyle that has implications far beyond what most Christians embody in their day-to-day lives. They are like the revolutionaries in Jesus' day who believed that his words had power, in simple but radical ways, to overturn the then-current form of Judaism, as well as the Roman Empire. These present-day revolutionaries also believe that it is possible to use the radical message of Jesus in any culture, time or situation. In a word, they are *hopefuls*. But not only are they hopeful, they question the current state of their religion.

I sat there wide-eyed, thinking, *These people were hopeful skeptics, and I have never heard of them.* Clarence Jordan, Jim Dowling, Ann Rampa and Toyohiko Kagawa are part of the Christian tradition, but we don't know about them and don't hear about them. Yet they are part of countercultural revolutions that embody peace and transformation, which are essential to understanding the life of Jesus.

Dave has collected story after story of these revolutionaries, and he tells some of them in his writings. That night he lent me a book he wrote called *Christi-Anarchy,* which talks about the role of Jesus in relation to empires, justice and how we should treat the marginalized. I couldn't help but think about the need for revolutionaries in the local church to overthrow some of the systems that are operating within our religious structures. But I also became hopeful because there are many things we can do as followers of the way of Jesus that can oppose some of the very same structures Jesus proposed we dismantle.

If we are to be followers of Jesus and if we want to emulate his life, then I believe that we must be like the many radical revolutionaries who've gone before us: we must take action against the hurtful power structures in the world and in the church. If we are not willing to call attention to systems of oppression where we see them, then we are not willing to completely follow the footsteps of Jesus.

This is part of what it means to be a hopeful skeptic. We question and are skeptical about current structures, but we are hopeful about the foundation of the structure and the possibilities of what can be built on that foundation. And we use this hope to produce change. So hope becomes action, in the same way that faith has to become action to be true faith.

A while ago I was rewatching *The Great Debaters* with some friends. The movie tells a story about the first African American debate team to become national champions. There are two patriarchal figures in the film; one was the debate teacher, played by Denzel Washington, and the other was the school's very religious headmaster, played by Forrest Whittaker. Denzel's character is hopeful for the black debate team, he is hopeful for his school, and he is even hopeful for the rights of a union of sharecroppers (a narrative subplot). But Forrest's headmaster is more a reserved and "pious" character.

At one point the headmaster tells Denzel's character that he should quietly submit to authority, and Denzel's character quips that Jesus was a radical who wouldn't be put in place by the authorities. When my one friend heard that, he muttered under his breath, "That isn't correct." And though I didn't follow up with him later, I took his comment to mean that he didn't see Jesus as a person who came to break down power systems. Similarly, many of us only see Jesus as a lamb who came to be slaughtered, as an offering to a God who demanded a perfect sacrifice. So we see in Jesus a person who lived a perfect life, a life that *must* have been congruent with being a perfect citizen and a perfect Jew.

But Jesus wasn't a perfect, low-key subject of Rome, nor was he a perfect Jew (at least in the eyes of the Jewish leaders around him!). In fact, these two groups put him to death precisely because they said he wasn't a faithful citizen or a faithful Jew. He broke the rules; he called society and the religious to reexamine the structures that they had created. While some people may think that those actions made him a better citizen or a more correct Jew, hopeful skeptics see in Jesus a person who was skeptical of the state of Judaism and who preached a hopeful message of change. And some of us are excited to follow his lead, knowing that if we want to follow him, change is what we must create.

THE POTENTIAL POWER OF A WELL-PLACED QUESTION

Back in 2007, I was talking to a friend of mine, Justin, who is from Alabama. He is an extremely creative artist, and because of his creative mind, he has thought of some interesting questions and ideas that I would love to see discussed in a faith community. He told me about a particular Sunday when the pastor of the church he was at started to describe, with a strong sense of conviction, a moral issue, and then the pastor had the audacity to pronounce that the way he had just presented the moral issue was the only possible way that God would view the issue.

Justin was extremely uncomfortable with what the pastor said because he and I tend to think that pronouncing any view as the *only* way God would see an issue is tantamount to heresy. This has to do with the idea that the ways of God are not the ways of humans, and Justin and I don't feel comfortable projecting anything onto the mind of God or claiming to have an exclusive grasp of the thoughts of God. So, as he expressed his feelings to me about the matter, I casually asked, "Why didn't you say something?"

He stared at me for a second and asked, "What? You mean afterward?"

"No," I said. "I mean don't be a jerk, but respectfully raise your hand next time. When a public speaker notices a raised hand in the audience, he or she will usually respond by asking what the question is. Then you respectfully ask if maybe there isn't another way to view the situation."

I think Justin was intrigued by that idea, by forcing the sermon to become conversational and thereby dismantling one of the structures that causes us such great skepticism about the institution. And an action like this would create space for others who have questions about the sermon's content as well. It would open the floor, and even the faith tradition itself, for questions.

Most pastors don't allow room for other people to comment on what they are preaching. They express their views, they defend their views, and they assume you are tracking along with them, but this seems a little one-sided. Perhaps these lectures on Sunday mornings are not what healthy communities need. Maybe they need discussion, action and openness.

So I don't know if Justin will raise his hand next time, but he needed to know that there are all sorts of options for either finding a community that will be fine with him raising his hand or changing the way his current community is structured so that they might allow dialogue at some point on a Sunday morning. Justin needed to recognize that his thoughts and voice, as a person in the assembly, are just as important as the voice of the person up front. This is a radical thought, but I believe that Jesus was all about radical thoughts and going against social norms. Jesus seemed to like the idea of mixed groups of people who would have had opposing points of view and styles of interaction. And Jesus also appears to have valued demonstrations in the religious institution, whether it be turning over tables or healing on the sabbath. Jesus seemed to bring the radical into the traditional to help broaden people's perspectives.

The weirdest thing about the suggestion I made to Justin is that it reflected a question that Leslie had asked me four years earlier when we were still dating and when she had just started attending formal church services after being away from the church for a while. She asked me why people couldn't question a pastor if they disagreed with him or her. Why couldn't they ask questions or object to statements during a sermon? Leslie, who hadn't been cultured into the church lifestyle, instinctively knew what it took me four years to figure out: you should start a dialogue when you have questions about things that are presented to you, and you should never accept anything just because someone with a microphone and a title says that it is from God.

Leslie knew, even then, that gatherings are most organic and most alive when there is more than one voice. Of course, I, as the good church worker, had quite a few answers, so I told her that those discussions and questions are meant for Sunday school, not for a sermon. I was at the same place as Justin: I understood the current church program to be set in stone and unmovable; it did not have any space for the "irreverent" people who wanted to challenge authority.

Over the next four years, though, I came to recognize how theologically important Leslie's question and the thoughts behind it were, especially if communities are to be authentic and open. Eventually, I realized that questioning has a place, even in a church service.

MONEY TALKS, GOD LISTENS

People who are hopeful for change will do their best to create it, and part of their hope for change comes simply from wondering if there might be a better way. I think my friend Kyle Martin demonstrates how questions and discussions produce changes in communities.

Kyle lives in Vancouver, and he also listens to my podcast. I got to meet up with him in the Bahamas at a learning party called Soularize, which was organized by The Ooze. We stood around one night talking about money. I was rambling on about my idea to shoot a documentary where I would go into churches and ask to see their budgets. Then, a la Michael Moore, I would point out all the things that the church uses its money on that don't help the community at all. I would be the whistleblower who shows that the majority of the money that churches take in stays inside the church and never feeds a hungry stomach or cures an infectious disease.

During this rambling conversation, Kyle expressed his own ideas about what he thought it meant to be a church in his community. And while I was thinking about becoming Michael Moore, Kyle got interested in seeing how far he could possibly go to be faithful with the way his own community budgets its finances. So, when he got home from this trip to the Bahamas, Kyle started making changes, and he managed to do what most community leaders do when they make drastic changes: he shrunk his community and lost some of his funding.

However, this didn't put too much of a kink in his plans, because he had already decided to shrink his funding by getting a full-time job outside of the faith community he worked in. But Kyle managed to restructure his community so that it now gives away 51 percent of its tithes to places outside of the church—and in the meantime, he works thirty-five to forty hours a week on the side, as well as coaches a community baseball team for fun. He does this so that his community can find a healthy way to live like Jesus together.

Kyle admits he is constantly working with the leaders at his church to reconfigure this experimental faith community, but he is determined to start putting values, like giving to the community, at the heart of the process. However, in order for his community to change, he had to buck the traditional models. When Kyle and I had talked about the idea of giving away 51 percent, we joked that the tagline behind this all would be, "If you aren't going to give God your all, will you at least give him the majority of it?"

Kyle became skeptical of the "script" that tells church leaders that tithes should stay in the church for church things, and he worked to redefine the tithing structure as a whole. This all happened, along with becoming less skeptical of churches and money, just by asking questions and having discussions.

Now admittedly Kyle's model is not one for growing huge mega-churches—and Kyle is okay with that—but this model of playing with tradition is cropping up everywhere. There are many hopefuls like Kyle who are changing their communities, however small or large, by testing the waters with different thoughts.

SO WHAT? NICE STORIES

You may think these are stories just used to fill up the pages of a book, but I think they are more than that. I think they are examples—not prescriptive examples to ensure a revolutionary-type of Christianity—that I hope get you to start thinking outside the traditional church structures and into a revolutionary mindset. Because if following Jesus doesn't produce a revolutionary lifestyle, then I would argue you aren't following the first-century Jesus. And even though I *say* these stories aren't prescriptive, I will dare you to raise your hand during a sermon, and I encourage you to fight for budget reform in your church, and I beg you to care for people that aren't like you.

I use the form of story because it is comfortable for me (it also seems like what Jesus did) and because I think stories help break us out of our normal modes of thinking. They get us to suspend our disbelief and to live vicariously through another person, they cause us to listen more than we would in normal conversation, and they can disarm us enough to show us a different perspective that we may not have been able to see before. I also think stories help us realign with the larger narrative of God by showing Jesus' cultural context and what he was working to embody, thus breaking people out of their current and possibly complacent perceptions.

Sometimes we don't see radical options like Kyle and his church's giving or Justin and his options for starting dialogue in the midst of a traditional service, because we aren't looking for these options, we are looking for labels. We are stuck in labeling. The church, especially in America, has a long tradition of labeling things and people as "sacred" or "secular." But we may have lost focus of the people Jesus surrounded himself with. When we forget that Jesus surrounded himself with scallywags, we usually end up defining what is "good" religion with "good" labels. Thus we regulate Jesus to a new Torah—not a new way but a new law. This makes us miss the point of his teachings, and oftentimes it makes us deemphasize our own heart and emphasize instead a labeling system of "dos" and "don'ts."

In the American South I sometimes say this to get a rise out of people: "We have to understand that the first miracle Jesus ever performed, if we believe the Gospel account is accurate, is buying top-shelf alcohol for a party that ran out of booze."

I get immediate blowback with this comment: "No, he didn't want to do the miracle; his mother made him. The story is about earthly obedience," or "He made nonalcoholic wine," or "You have to understand the significance of the miracle in its cultural context, it is really a jab at the Bacchus, the Roman god of wine and intoxication." Maybe those things are true, but what is also true is that Jesus was constantly questioning the labeling system that had been put in place by the current religious structure, and he was challenging it. More than once he and his followers were accused of either *being* drunkards or *at least* associating with them.

Sometimes we need to hear things in a slightly different way to understand the importance of Jesus. Jesus didn't live and die to tell us if it was moral or immoral to drink wine, and this miracle story should shock us out of that perception in the same way that a raised hand in a sermon would shock the community into asking why no one has ever raised his or her hand before. It seems that Jesus wanted his movement to comprise a countercultural group of people who push against the current systems and bring the kingdom of heaven to earth in the here and now. This kingdom looked diverse and, apparently, had parties with wine.

If Jesus had wanted to show submission to authority, he would have joined a Jewish sect and toed the party line. But his subversive life challenged the religious structures, basically by throwing parties or by showing up at them. It started with a wedding and moved on to tax collectors' houses or places with prostitutes; it turned to an upper room and ended on a beach with fresh-cooked fish. It also included the unequal members of society like women or minorities and even a Zealot-turned-traitor. It is probably safe to assume that these members of Jesus' group had different ideas of what the kingdom of heaven would look like: for women, it may have looked like equal rights, for the Zealots it looked like Roman blood, and for minorities it meant a place at the table. *Those* are the prescriptive stories: you should bring wine to a wedding; you should dine with those not like you.

When I read these stories, I start to think that we have the wrong people in our churches. I think a church should be more like a party: parties are conversational gatherings with all kinds of people. They may start out with a few select friends, but news gets around, and before you know it you have the friends of friends of friends and the freeloaders. But our churches today are gatherings of people who don't always turn out to be as diverse as a full-on party.

Please don't think that these parties aren't going on somewhere. In fact, they are very much happening. And, like I have said, the institutional church isn't an evil place, but every institution needs a little revolution and a little civil disobedience.

9

Communities That Give Hope

IT DOESN'T TAKE TOO MUCH SEARCHING to start bumping into hundreds of online communities or websites that give even the biggest church-basher a bit of hope.

These new expressions of community—whether they are house churches, emergent churches, coffee-house gatherings or just plain, old book clubs—are typically not composed of people that have been formally excommunicated from a church. And they aren't usually made up of individuals who have put in a formal resignation of membership with the old institution. They are just new expressions of an existing faith and of existing communities.

Those critical of these new faith expressions, or small groups gathering under a new name, express their concerns about these emerging faith communities as questions about oversight, accountability or their apparent lack of structure. The critical see these new gatherings as composed of lone gunmen who are isolating themselves from the larger faith community and are probably straying in doctrine. Yet in spite of attacks from critics, these communities actually try to keep close ties with other communities and work to create systems of accountability.

These are the communities that give me hope, inspire me and confirm for me that the future of Christianity will be as different and as vibrant as it was in the first two or three centuries.

MICRONATIONS

The biggest criticism of new faith communities is that they are isolationists. Maybe they didn't agree with their old church, so the outside perception is that they up and left, and couldn't care less about anything except a new small group where they can do whatever they want. However, most emerging communities are not like that at all.

In fact, I have only seen one real example that would fit that criticism, and it wasn't some new faith community: it was a group of old ladies who used to stand outside of a Baptist church my family used to attend in Virginia. I don't remember anything about why they were doing what they were doing, but I knew they used to be members of our Baptist church. One day they left and started carrying signs that accused our church of whatever they were upset about. Every Sunday they would be there, looking nice and carrying signs, which mostly said "Hooray" for their side.

That is the only example I can think of where a group decided it didn't want to be a part of a community so it formed an anticommunity. I have heard of church splits, where two sides go separate ways, and I know that they are out there, but these emerging faith communities don't seem to fit that category on the whole. They don't seem to be anticommunities but rather healthy communities that are committed to change and discipleship.

The problem comes, though, when people consider the communities that are sprouting as micronations. Micronations are a relatively new phenomenon, but they have probably existed since the dawn of humanity. The basic idea is something like this: At some point in a particular kind of man's life (yes, most micronations are run by men), he chooses to separate himself from society. Not unlike Thoreau's *Walden*, this particular man wants to declare the place he is dwelling as a nation of its own. Such a man will find uninhabited land—a loft in England, a small island, a barge or a territory not yet claimed by a government—and will claim this place for himself, of course, naming himself a ruler. This has happened throughout history, but with almost every square inch of the world having been claimed now, it has become a rarer phenomenon. Travel around enough, though, and you will bump into a couple.

Micronations don't get much recognition, perhaps because publicity itself could help establish them as legitimate. The most popular micronation would have to be the Principality of Sealand, which is an old antiaircraft platform off the southeast coast of England. The principality has successfully defended its right to exist against the British government, Spanish pirates and a few internal insurrections.*

I don't know why Sealand is so cool to me, but the idea of this monolithic piece of concrete jutting out of the sea and being claimed by a British guy who had enough vision for the place that he would defend it is awesome. There are stories of him firing cannons over the bow of the British Navy, and suddenly, it feels like we have entered the land of pirates again. In fact, Roy Bates, the pirate radio broadcaster-cum-royalty is the monarch of the micronation, and he has successfully minted coins, printed passports and established nobility.

I could write for pages about micronations because I find them fascinating for some reason. All of this to say, I've found these micronations all around, and they seem to be exactly what some people are accusing new faith expressions of being—societies that want to divorce themselves from everyone outside.

From here to there. Aside from micronations being interesting, I think they highlight some of the aspects of new faith expressions and some of the criticisms. As I mentioned, the largest criticism levied

---

*Its sordid history can be found on online if you are keen for a more descriptive tale.

against new faith communities is that they are born out of an isolationist spirit. The idea is that, like Whangamomona, there was some dispute, and a group of people just left the larger community, together declaring a new leader and new rules.

This definitely happens when a church splits and it occasionally happens in some other start-up churches or new faith communities. However, the kind of communities that I am seeing crop up all over the world, which are doing new and inspiring things, aren't typically born out of a separatist spirit. These communities are trying to meet needs outside of the ones that were met in the old communities. These communities value smaller numbers because they can become more intimate and more sustaining. They are communities of hope who are not erecting new borders but are trying to start new life while keeping their old connections—even their traditional connections, which they respect because they were born out of those traditions.

Until recently these communities haven't received much press because they are typically small in number and don't advertise themselves the way larger churches can. You have to look for them if you want to find them; they blend into the culture they inhabit, operating in subtle ways and conspiring to change things for the better. I find hope in the fact that these communities exist, that they are out there and doing it. I respect that. These communities give me hope for the church at large, because it seems that there are more and more of these communities cropping up—and even though they are small, they are becoming more numerous. I see people like me, and some unlike me, doing things that I want to do and, following Gandhi's suggestion, being the change they want to see in the world.

COMMUNITIES OF HOPE

These communities are different from micronations in that they aren't started by the very person who wants to rule and in that they don't elect new leaders to replace their old ones. Rather, they usually have opportunities for all involved to help with leading and facilitating. I described micronations so that you could get a picture of an isolationist community, and as I go on to describe some of these communities that give me hope, I want you to decide if those communities are really isolationist or if they deserve to be listed among the millions of other communities of faith.

A few of these communities that I have had the chance to visit and that have inspired me are The Waiters Union of West End in Brisbane, Australia; Black Star Coffee in Brisbane; Kiva and other microlenders; and the mobile community established by the traveling troubadours of The Cobalt Season.

The Waiters Union. West End is nestled in an area that has been cut away from the center of Brisbane by the curves of the Brisbane River. It has a deep history for those living there now and for the aboriginal Australians who have met in its Musgrave Park for generations.

This community—with its older homes, a few trendy, countercultural coffee klatches and its homeless population—teams with life. In this area Dave Andrews initiated an incredible community project called The Waiters Union, which is described as "a network of residents in West End who are committed to developing a sense of community in the locality with our neighbours, including those who are marginalised, in the radical tradition of Jesus of Nazareth."* The Waiters Union is more a commitment to valuing the marginalized than a weekly ministry. Therefore, it is hard to tell what parts of Dave's schedule are Waiters Union activities or just his personal life, like when he's out eating with people in West End. He and his family believe that to reflect the life of Jesus, they must be *among* the community. So Dave lives in the heart of it: he knows his neighbors, he knows the shopkeepers, he knows the homeless, the poor and the mentally challenged who live in the hostels. And everyone knows Dave.

---

*Taken from The Waiters Union website at <www.waitersunion.org>.

I can only speak about the events that I have attended, but using those, I will try to give you an idea of how Dave's version of Christlike community looks. Every fortnight (that is how you say "every two weeks" when you are in an area that has been influenced by the British), Dave and The Waiters Union throw a dinner party. They meet on the ground floor of a local Anglican church, aptly named Saint Andrew's. There is a crew that sets up tables with tablecloths and sometimes candles, and pretty soon a procession starts toward the food. Some of the staff, or "waiters" of The Waiters Union, as well as some of the attendees bring food and drinks to have a common meal. The attendees are bussed in by passenger van or taxi from apartment complex to hostel to apartment complex, picking up all who want to make it out for the night. These people are members of the community who are poor or homeless or mentally disabled, but when they arrive at the church, there is no distinction between them and the members of The Waiters Union. Everyone is treated equally and valued as a member of the common table. Each week new friendships are made and old ones are strengthened.

The meal is only one part of Dave's community, but he and his family also open up their house to outsiders. Travelers, distressed locals and church groups can all be found in his home on any given day. Dave also fights for the rights of the renters in his community and organizes dynamic community dialogues.* In addition to these dinners and conversations, Dave also seemed to be a human trafficker—in a good way. Dave and his wife, Angie, noticed that refugees from Africa were trying to immigrate into the community and needed help flying their family members to Australia, so the Andrewses set up a system of loans to establish a way to get refugees into Australia safely. Commu-

---

*One dialogue I attended was an interfaith discussion about faith traditions and how they shaped community values. It was a warm and open talk with local Muslims, a Hindu, a Tibetan Buddhist and a handful of Christians, and it didn't end with a prayer of salvation from anyone!

nity, justice and openness seem to be the common thread in The Waiters Union activities.

Dave's daughter and son-in-law, Evonne and Marty, also work with The Waiters Union and the community of West End. They have started their own community initiative, which are grassroots companies that employ immigrants and others in need. Among their initiatives are a "green" pest-control service and a coffee shop, Blackstar Coffee.

Blackstar Coffee. Blackstar Coffee has its values painted on the wall of the shop in the shape of a five-point star. The values, one at each point of the star, are specialty coffee, community economics, social enterprise, organic, fair trade. Those are the values set up by this company.

Marty and Evonne have created their own community in the midst of West End. They provide organic, fair-trade coffee to the community, and they hire workers who need employment. These workers might be immigrants or single moms or others who would have a problem getting a job elsewhere. They aren't driven by the green/organic fad; they are driven to create an ethical community that serves the rest of the community at large. And they have created a fresh expression of what it might look like to live like Jesus in the community of Brisbane.

Kiva. Though not a Christian organization, Kiva (kiva.org) has become a source of inspiration, not only to those who are logged in and part of it but also to the thousands of people and communities it empowers. Kiva is an online community created by Jessica and Michael Flannery. The husband-and-wife team combined Jessica's background in microfinance and Michael's experience as a programmer for Silicon Valley startups (the likes of which include TiVo) to create a way to use the Internet to get money to poor individuals abroad who would like to start businesses in the communities that they live.

Kiva allows us to learn about people all over the world, and connects us with friends we already know. We can invite friends to join with us in loaning, or we can give a gift certificate to others for them to loan. With a minimum donation of $25, users can browse profiles of individuals living in poverty but trying to make a difference. As a lender, we receive updates on how the business that we help fund is doing and how well the loan is being paid back. The Flannerys have established a very low-interest loan system that funds these businesses, and the businesses provide jobs and services for the same low-income community that the owner of the business lives in.

I have used Kiva a handful of times to lend money to entrepreneurs. Miguel, for example, lives in Danli, Honduras, and runs a mobile dairy shop, carrying milk, cheese and butter throughout the community to sell. Miguel was able to use the money that I and others lent to him to strengthen his business by buying more necessities to provide to others and make a profit for his family. He has completely paid the loan back. Mrs. Seng is a baker in Cambodia, and her loan helps her to expand her business and employ others around her. She is working on paying back her loan right now. These are the people that I am making online connections with. I will probably never physically meet them, but Kiva allows me to help them.

When Jessica Flannery was on our podcast, she told Josh that the vision of Kiva is to "connect people through lending for the purpose of poverty alleviation"—and they are doing just that. They have worked with other groups in multiple countries to gather lists of possible business owners and have created profiles for each possible owner in order to give online users the option to start funding these businesses with only a few clicks of a mouse. Jessica also stated that one of her biggest priorities is to empower women around the globe and establish these underprivileged women as business owners.[*] Thanks to the effort of this married couple that is happening.

Not more than two weeks after we aired the podcast on the web,

[*] The interview Josh had with Kiva is still available on our podcast website: "Kiva: Jessica Jackley," The Nick and Josh Podcast, episode 4.8, September 3, 2007 <http://thenick-andjoshpodcast.com/2007/09/03/podcast-version-48>.

Kiva.org filled every single possible loan profile they had on their site. Josh claims this has something to do with our listener base and The-Nick-and-Josh-Podcast Listener Army, but we both know it had more to do with the fact that Jessica and Michael were on Oprah the same week.

This combination of online networking and microlending institutions gives me hope. I have been in churches that have started the same sort of microlending programs with communities that they work with outside of the country, and the more I hear about these groups, the more hopeful I become about the power communities have to produce positive change in the world.

The Cobalt Season. Ryan and Holly Sharp have a music group called The Cobalt Season (thecobaltseason.com). The Sharps have spent some time as gypsies, where they throw everything into a car and travel around to share their music with new friends. It would be wrong to call what they do a ministry because it lacks much of the structure of a ministry, but also because I don't think they would categorize themselves as such; it could also be wrong to classify them as a band because they aren't in the music business. Instead, it may be most accurate to say that they cultivate experiences by telling stories through the medium of music in communities where they travel. You may think that this description is a bit pedantic, but if you think about the difference between experiencing music in your own home with your friends versus going to a concert hall or stadium, perhaps you can respect the distinction.

Early on, the Sharps decided that they didn't want to be part of the "music industry," nor did they want to try to make a lot of money doing what they love. Rather, they just wanted to share their songs with friends, so they decided to only play music in people's houses—usually people that they would also stay with while they were in town. Their gatherings are small and intimate, and you can even feel that intimacy in the live recordings that they've done from their house shows.

Listening to the background on why the Sharps operate this way and believing that what they are doing is creating a new expression of community gives me hope for the new and creative ways that people are finding to gather and tell stories and encourage each other. The idea that there is a couple traveling and small communities gathering, presenting and being presented with thoughtful songs to contemplate together, is hope-producing and inspiring to me, because they are asking the same questions I am asking and they are putting them elegantly into song.

HOPE IN FRESH EXPRESSIONS

I have only listed a few communities here and have tried to keep my list to communities that I have personally interacted with. Although there are many others that give me hope, I haven't experienced them to a large extent, but there are other groups that I know of out there, and I've have had the occasion to become somewhat familiar with them through conferences or the podcast. Some other communities that you might consider include Karen Sloan's monastic prayer community in Pittsburgh, Formation House (http://formationhouse.org), Pete Rollins's eclectic community Ikon (www.ikon.org.uk), or the online group Off The Map (http://offthemap.com).

These communities that I've mentioned are only a few examples of that I believe have no isolationist threads in their fabric. They have created something new that they saw a need for, while at the same time being members of a larger tradition that came before them. These communities give me hope. They don't require huge budgets or a large following; they are simple groups meeting around basic values. There are other communities like this out there. They don't necessarily have to be new expressions of faith meeting in low-lit coffee houses, but they can sprout up in what look like traditional churches.

My mentor from my early years of youth ministry is now the head pastor at his own church. I visited him one night to experience his Sunday evening service. It was in a typical church building and was definitely part of a congregation, but the way he conducted the service itself made it seem like I was at a gathering of a small group of people with a healthy innovative ethos. After his conversational message, where people would sometimes speak out and try to finish sentences or offer up thoughts, he asked if there were any questions or comments about what he had discussed. I listened as a discussion time commenced that took about the same amount of time as his message. While I sat and listened, I realized that it was not just in the new faith communities where I can find hope but also in denominational churches, with congregations that have deep histories themselves.

Whether in the new communities that I've spent most of this chapter describing or in the old communities that have accepted new forms of worship, I am hopeful about the future of faith communities, especially those that emphasize dialogue and humility.

10

Prayer

IS THERE ANYBODY OUT THERE?

IN MAKING THE LIST OF THINGS that I am skeptical of and things that I am hopeful for, it was like sitting in my apartment before our world trip, sifting through my things. I had these two metaphorical boxes, one with "hopeful" written on the top and one with "skeptical" written on it. Some items I tossed back and forth. I wanted to put Scripture as hopeful, but I was skeptical of how it is handled—so I decided against it. Throughout this book, I explained which box most of my ideas have ended up in, but I still had one large item to figure out how to pack: prayer.

Prayer was a sticky one. It was something that I had cut down on in the previous years, and I had no idea how much I planned on using it while abroad. Still, I needed to figure out where put this monolithic possession. I knew I wasn't going to scrap it, but I had to pick a box. While establishing what I was hopefully skeptical about, I thought about all the actual science fiction stuff that I had packed up, and one of the things I packed when we left our apartment in Birmingham was a magazine clipping that talked about a golden record.

THE GOLDEN RECORD

In 1977 there were two golden records minted that would never be mass produced. The value of these two records would probably be astronomical if you ever got your hands on them, which you won't. Because they are the Voyager Golden Records. These records were produced for the sole purpose of being placed on the Voyager space probes, and they were intended for use by extraterrestrial life.

The records were meant to be compilations of humanity, sent out and hopefully played by another race of creatures in the cosmos. A committee at NASA, which was chaired by Carl Sagan, compiled the content. Don't expect an answer from far off any time soon. The records will have to travel on the Voyager for 40,000 years (now only about 39,969) before it will even reach our closest star, Alpha Centauri.

The set list for this record contained a variety of sound clips and music, ranging from the Brandenburg Concerto No. 2 in F major to "Johnny B. Goode" by Chuck Berry. In addition, there was a collection of voices and sounds from all over the globe. Then-President Jimmy Carter even recorded a message saying, "This is a present from a small, distant world, a token of our sounds, our science, our images, our music, our thoughts and our feelings. We are attempting to survive our time so we may live into yours." The records also have a binary code etched on one side of them, giving instructions on how to play the recording, as well as a diagram showing the location of our sun, another diagram of the hydrogen atom, an image of a man and woman and some other etchings.

These records were part of an ongoing search for life outside our solar system. In 1960, SETI (or the Search for Extra-Terrestrial Intelligence) started searching the sky to find transmissions that might be sent our way from other planets. Frank Drake started these experiments, searching for any transmissions pointed in our direction. There have been blips here and there that seemed to be transmissions of some sort, but nothing too conclusive.

Regardless of the lack of confirmation, we are still searching. In 1999, Seti@home was launched and five million people in over two hundred countries donated part of their computer processors' power to help decode the constant string of information that the SETI project continuously receives from space. Someone had the innovative idea to get the public involved and allow anyone with some computer downtime and an Internet connection to donate their personal computers to help with the unusually large task of sifting through the massive amounts of information. To date, it looks as though nineteen billion hours of computer processing time has been accomplished with outside help. Regrettably, we don't have any big news yet.

Are you still with me? Or have you dropped the book and started playing the *X-Files* theme with that cool 1980 Casio from your closet? Perhaps I should throw off my sci-fi sensibilities and move back to the topic of prayer, which I think, oddly enough, is related.

Prayer. In the Bible we have two "first" accounts of prayer. One is in the creation narrative, where God and Adam talk, and I guess God addresses Eve too (at least he does during the curse). So let's just say that we have God talking to man and woman, but the only part of this that we might call prayer is when Adam would walk and talk with God in the Garden of Eden. That was the intimate conversational time with the divine.

Then humanity was removed from the Garden and, I assume, due to lack of transportation they stayed in the region near the Garden. In this creation narrative, the Garden seems to possess a thin place in the world where God and humanity connect. It is around this region that Cain and Abel might have still talked to God as well, but after that whole killing debacle Cain left the presence of the Lord and settled in a land called Nod (Genesis 4:16). It would seem that the connection with God was lost since Cain decidedly left God's presence.

Then there is a peculiar verse a few verses, and presumably a couple generations, later that simply says, "At that time, people began to call on the name of the LORD" (Genesis 4:26). With this little statement, one part of a verse, we have the birth of prayer outside of Eden, and this discipline now lies at the epicenter of every religion.

We don't get background; we could assume that since the exit of the Garden, God and humans did not communicate in the intimate manner of the garden walks. We read pieces of the story where God talks to Cain or Abel, but we don't read humans invoking the presence of the Lord through prayer until the grandson of Adam and Eve is on the scene.

Prayer confuses me. Maybe you are wondering why such a seemingly simple concept and spiritual practice confuses me, but it just does. I went to a local bookstore while living in Taupo, New Zealand, and I counted fifteen books on prayer. This was not even at a Christian bookstore or a Books-a-Million in the American Bible belt! And along with the fifteen Christian books I counted, there were others that could be classified as prayer in nontraditional ways, including books on meditation, chanting and a variety of other transcendental and shamanistic practices.

It seems that everyone has some sort of opinion or advice on talking to God. Some books advise repeating ancient Scripture to call God to task on promises he once made. Other books give advice on how to discern the voice of God. And while I have read about a dozen books on prayer, I haven't gotten much more out of these books than lessons in what to say when you pray and how to pray more. These books read like self-help books, but none of them seem to actually help me "hear" God.

The truth is that I have never "heard" the voice of God, nor have I ever met a single person who was convinced that he or she had heard the voice of God in an audible manifestation—the kind that, if a third party were present, they would have heard it audibly as well.

Many people describe hearing from God in one of these ways: (1)

getting a peaceful feeling about something they are uncertain about, (2) finding a Bible verse that speaks to a situation that they are in, or (3) having a new and inspiring idea or perspective that seems to come from outside themselves. And I have described prayer in all of these ways throughout my life. I have found things in the Bible or I have felt something that seemed to come from outside of me, and I would attribute that verse or feeling to God.

The tricky thing about the subject of prayer is that nothing I say about it can be proven or disproven, empirically speaking. That fact makes prayer difficult. Who can say that inklings I have or thoughts I think are spoken to me are not from God? And who hasn't seen articles in trustworthy magazines, such as the *Time*, that have stories of independent studies showing better medical outcomes are more common for people who pray? Or what about the successful people who claim prayer as their secret for success?

The hopeful side of me likes to think that the divine communicates with me personally, but there is that pesky, skeptical part of me that wonders to what extent I can trust my own thoughts—especially when I think my thoughts are divine words.

What I do know is that no Scripture was ever written for the sole audience of Nick Fiedler, for the exact situations that I encounter in the present. I can't put a metext on prayer. The Bible is a voice, but it is not a personal line from God to Nick. It is a combination of books written to many people, over a couple thousand years. And in the same way that the Constitution of the United States can answer a court question about the legality of a present action, it cannot operate like a Magic 8 Ball and respond to questions it was never designed to answer—unless they are about the Constitution itself or the constitutionality of an action.

In the same way that the Magic 8 Ball can only answer questions framed to it within a given context (including, mostly, questions with yes-or-no answers, I cannot ask in prayer the exact date of my death or the meaning of my life (well I could, but the closest answer I would get is "outcome does not look good"). In this same sense, the Constitution is not conversational, nor necessarily is the Bible.

All of that to say: I don't think that my interaction with the voice of Scripture is a personal interaction with the voice of God *in the present*. I could definitely use the language to say that a verse is "speaking to me," but the idea that a present God is conversing with me in this moment doesn't flesh with the idea that something written long ago is transcending time. So, out of the three options that I proposed of how people understand prayer, this option of God speaking through Scripture isn't working for me.

If I take the scriptural aspect out of the mix, then my thoughts about prayer are limited to my feelings of peace or an inaudible voice in my head. But how do I know what is divine peace or what thoughts are divine? Think of the story of Abraham, where God asked Abraham to sacrifice his son Isaac.

Imagine with me for a second that people in Scripture prayed the same way we do and imagine that they didn't get an audible voice. It *is* possible that they didn't always hear an audible voice; I mean, we don't get audible God-voices right now, yet we still use the biblical language of "hearing God" or "talking with God." I know that in some stories we are to understand that the voice of God is audible; Moses was said to talk to God in the same way that we would talk to a friend (Exodus 33:11), so in some cases God apparently spoke audibly.

But for the sake of being hypothetical, what if Abraham didn't get an audible voice? What if him "hearing from God" was just like it is for us, when we're on our beds at night, staring at the dark ceiling and having thoughts move through our minds? Now what if you heard a voice in your head that told you to kill a family member? What if it was specific? It would sort of be like you were Jack Nicholson in *The Shining,* hearing that voice telling him to kill his family. (In fact, rent *The Shining* and imagine that the voices and visions in the movie are of divine origin; then have your Bible study talk about that in context of the Abraham story. How awesome would that be?)

What kind of dedication would it take to give everything you have to an inaudible voice? Imagine the story of Abraham happening like prayer happens now; imagine that he didn't get to hear an audible voice. I think about that story anytime that I think I "hear" the voice of God, and I wonder if I would be as sure as Abraham was. I wonder, *Is it really God that I am hearing?* If I were hearing that exact same "voice" telling me to do something that could cost a life, would I do it? Would you? How much do you trust that voice that you call God?

I think about these questions all the time, like, Did people during Old Testament times really hear the voice of God in an audible way? Did Jesus cut out the audio when he came to earth and died? Since humanity received a physical incarnation of God, do we no longer get the audible voice? I understand that, to some seasoned Christians, these are really lame questions. These Christians may believe that in the Old Testament God spoke audibly, but today God's voice is inaudible (with the exception of some charismatics who may think they hear an audible voice)—and that is just the way it is. But I can't see things that cut and dry, and stop my questions.

Fortunately, I did find some biblical stories that make me feel a little more secure when I don't completely understand prayer. Do you remember the story about the disciples picking a new disciple after the death of Judas? With Judas's betrayal and subsequent suicide, there was an opening in the Twelve, and the remaining eleven had to choose a new member. I find their method for picking the new member interesting. They had two people in mind, and to choose the right one, they prayed to God and asked God to reveal the correct one. And then —they gambled (Acts 1:24-26).

Okay, so it was called casting lots. It was what the soldiers were doing for Jesus' clothes (Matthew 27:35). And, in the same way that some soldier could have taken home Jesus' cloak, a new number twelve was picked. What perplexes me about this story is that we have these eleven men who spent between one and three years with Jesus; Jesus was their teacher, and he even taught them about prayer. Yet instead of solely praying about this decision or instead of listening for the voice of God, they gambled, with the assumption that God would direct the lots.

I wonder if they questioned the answers they got when they were praying. Did they need something definitive so the group wouldn't argue about the outcome? Why would these followers of Jesus use this technique? Should I use it? Certainly we never read that Jesus used this. What are we to make from this story?

There was a similar device used by the priests in Israel; it was part of a breastplate that could somehow be used to discern the will of God. We don't know too much about this, but we know that when the Ark of the Covenant was built, there was also a breastplate that the priest was to wear when he approached the Ark. In the breastplate were two stones called the Urim and Thummim (Exodus 28:30). The breastplate seemed to be used to communicate with God when both stones and the lid of the Ark of the Covenant (also known as the mercy seat) were in close proximity, and God's presence was said to be between the cherubim on the Ark (Exodus 25:22).

Later we read that the Urim and Thummim could be consulted (Ezra 2:63), and Saul used the Urim to get answers to questions— though he sometimes did not get an answer, just like with his dreams or with the prophets (1 Samuel 28:6). In fact, because the Saul could not get an answer from the Lord, he consulted a witch because he needed a physical and audible answer from someone or something (1 Samuel 28:7-14). No one knows exactly what the Urim or Thummim were, but they appear to have been a way to communicate with God. Some scholars postulate that this method was similar to casting lots, in that perhaps the stones were cast onto the ark in some way. Although, the one thing we know is that, even in the Old Testament, people were looking for tangible answers to their prayers.

I don't blame the people for doing it. I need answers that I can hold, or I need a voice, or I need a lot more than I get. But just knowing that the people of the Old Testament, and the followers of Jesus, not only needed to learn how to pray but they still doubted their own prayers— to the extent that, at least once, they needed to cast lots—makes me hopeful. Those stories make me feel like my doubt and skepticism are shared with others in the Christian tradition.

The truth is, even with my skeptical side, I find prayer transcendental. Before meals I see the importance of developing a thankful attitude—and not in comparing myself to the starving and using their suffering to feel better about my own status; no, just in being thankful that my needs are met. When thinking about important life decisions, I study the teachings of those who've gone before me, I study Jesus, and I even ask the clichéd question, What would Jesus do? And when there are people in need, I ask God for change for them, and I work to convert the hope of "change" into personal action.

I don't know if my thoughts on prayer are correct. And, really, when it comes to theology, I am just packing and labeling boxes—being skeptical and hopeful. I just wonder how prayer works in a time when the population does not hear audibly from God, and I wonder how other hopeful skeptics try to separate their personal thoughts from divine thoughts.

Where does that leave me? In this case, I am in the hopeful camp. Prayer is a central tenant in all the major religions. It seems to be a "centering" act that can bring our thoughts from all aspects of our scattered lives into a divine space. When engaging in prayer is not self-centered and selfish at heart, it can be the most helpful part of someone's life. When I have to make an important decision, my first inclination is to make a quick decision. My second inclination is to act out of self-preservation. But what I have been trying to do is use prayer as a selfless centering act. When I do this, I make the best decisions. I think it is the same for most of us.

During my last year of high school and my first year of college, I had a great Sunday school facilitator. He was my favorite Sunday school teacher—and not just because I hated the idea of Sunday school and he saved me from that dread by creating a good class experience—and he was really good at forming the time we spent. There is a pivotal Patrick Morley quote that he centered much of our time and discussion around: "There is a God we want, and a God that is. And they are not the same God. The turning point in our lives is when we stop seeking the God we want and start seeking the God who is."*

So I admit it: I pray a lot less than I used to. In fact, I have cut out a lot of my prayer when it is asking for something. I think that the way we talk to God shows what type of God we think we have. It seems like talking to God, to a lot of us, has become about checking items off a shopping list or trying to withdrawal money from a huge, corporate bank account.

When I am sick or need money, a job, or anything else, I have stopped bringing such issues to God as requests. I don't want my interaction with the divine to be one that is asking for personal favors all the time. I have come to think that when I constantly pray just to ask for things, it is as if I have a really good friend and during the majority of our conversations I ask for things—help with something I am doing, money, a job. The truth is, though, I hope that even in my casual relationships I am seen as someone who gives and contributes more than someone who asks. I never want to be seen as a taker, someone who's constantly asking for things. I think about prayer the same way.

Josh Ritter has a line in the song "Girl in the War," which is off his monumental album *The Animal Years,* where he sings, "Talking to God is Laurel beggin Hardy for a gun." I have never asked Josh Ritter if he

---

*Patrick Morley, *Seven Seasons of the Man in the Mirror* (Grand Rapids: Zondervan, 2002), p. 184.

was referring to consumeristic prayer, but perhaps he is giving us a picture of a situation that might not end well. Perhaps, when we turn the central tenet of every faith into merely a shopping list of requests for the divine—some of which we will get and some of which we will never find—maybe that is a scene that would be funny if it weren't also so tragic.

Now, not everyone prays about stuff they want all the time, but for me to not be skeptical of prayer, I not only have to listen to the direction of God but I have to make sure that I am not concentrating too hard on my selfish reasoning or my own thoughts. The best way for me to accomplish that is by taking out all of my asking. Since I have taken out the asking part of prayer, I now use prayer as a time to become more centered on the things that I believe God wants me to be centered on—the poor, the needy, the hurting and the community around me. Perhaps prayer is the best time to center ourselves on the things of God instead of trying to bring God into our small situations (like getting that parking space).

The difference for me when I pray is that I consider what *I* need to *do,* how I need to take action, and I hope that my mind being centered on God will give me the inspiration to do the things that God would want done. Prayer then becomes a hopeful act, because the hope that I have becomes action.

BACK TO E.T.

After all of this, I come back to my thoughts about the search for extraterrestrial life. In some ways I often feel that praying is a gamble. If we were to actually believe like the ancients that God resides in the heavens, we would know that he must be more than a billion light years away since we can't see him.

However, I think most of us have settled on the notion that God does not exist in our dimension or physical realm, so each prayer I offer feels a bit like sending a Voyager probe into a porthole to another dimension—with the hope it will be received and played.

I hold onto the goodness of prayer like I hold onto the goodness of exploring the cosmos. I hold onto prayer with a deep belief that there is someone on the other end, and that in trying to make a connection, I am reaching inside and outside of myself to experience the God of creation. Another infamous Christian bumper sticker is the "Prayer changes things" one, and though the belief and theology behind it are is fine, I would prefer one that says "Prayer changes *people*." I am, indeed, hopeful that prayer can change things, but I believe that the biggest thing that prayer changes is the person praying. And that is the main reason I am hopeful about prayer.

I can't think of a better example for the way that prayer changes a person than the story of when my dad became my dad. My dad is not my biological father, and the details of the entire story aren't pertinent except for the fact that my mom remarried a great guy who I not only call my dad but who has been and always will be my dad. My sister and I were young at the time when my dad became Dad to us, but we understood exactly what was going on. My mom and dad were college sweethearts who had gone separate ways, but they ended up back together, soon to be married. My dad was (and is) crazy about my mom, but he was unsure of how the whole kids aspect would work out—not because he was against the idea but because it was a complicated situation. What would we call him? How would we respond to him? Would we get along? All of that. He realized that he would not only be marrying my mother but also her two children.

Concerned about the complications that would come in the relationship, he prayed and prayed and prayed, and pleaded with God to put the love in him so that he would feel that love as if my sister and I were his own. And the almost-impossible happened: that loved formed inside him. After my mom married him, it has been like he was always my dad. My sister and I were legally adopted, and we changed our last names to his. I even changed my middle name to his middle name. Almost instantly, a new family was forged together without the drama that typically comes in similar situations. The family came together in a strong way, and there was never any divisiveness between us. Even to this day, we have never had a fight where I've yelled, "You aren't my real dad!" In fact, we have rarely had any type of argument.

When I think about this scenario, I can't help but be hopeful about the transformational power of prayer. As a hopeful skeptic, I pray in the same way that my dad did. I pray for changes in myself, and I pray that I will be filled with the love of God. Prayer has that power, I think; the stuff of transformation seems to be in its very fabric. Of course, when it comes to guidance or questions, I am always open to an audible encounter or bidding on eBay for Urim and Thummim or first-century sets of lots, and I would be happy to put such a purchase to daily use.

11

Conclusions and Concert T-Shirts

I HAVE COVERED A VARIETY OF RELATED and unrelated topics while dissecting my life into the two categories of "hopeful" and "skeptical"—while at the same time separating myself from the overall traditional label of "Christian." Online religion, space probes, alien life, praying with some sort of breastplate, Facebook, Wikipedia, sex changes in Scripture, world travel, Jesus bumper stickers, paying for a lawyer's services in beer and all the rest. Where does this whimsical, disjointed journey leave us? Are you, the reader, and I, the writer, more disoriented than when we started to think about all of these things? What *really* is the purpose of this journey? Am I trying to get you all to be followers of a new way of thinking? Am I trying to get you to leave your church? Forsake your childhood faith?

Not at all.

For me, this book started when I sat in my apartment, trying to pack up some beliefs. However, I discovered that my beliefs don't have to neatly fit into the categories of *either* "hopeful" *or* "skeptical." In fact, I have a brand new label maker to use during the process. So if I had a major intention for this book, it would be that my packing might serve as a small catalyst to keep you asking difficult questions and interacting deeply with them. I would want you to challenge what doesn't seem to fit or work or make sense to you. I would want you to see that we possibly have more options today than ever before when it comes to our lives and faith.

So for those of us that would strive to be like Jesus but are done with the church or institutional Christianity, I would want to strongly suggest to you that with all these options, you don't have to drop Jesus or write off the entire Bible—even if you don't believe that the Bible came to us in perfect, written form via the mouth of God. Instead, we have options, so we don't have to move to the *exact opposite* of the belief that doesn't work for us.

Many of us have options to travel, we have vocational options, and we have many options as to what we believe. Not only do we have many options on what to believe, we have many great, logical and scripturally based options as to what to believe. There is rarely, if ever, a single perfect belief on our planet. So when you get to that snag in your personal beliefs, you don't have to jump to the polar opposite position. If you find an error in your version of Scripture, you don't have to declare Scripture to be worthless. If you find that you doubt the complexities of God, you don't have to become an atheist.

Faith and religion, as most things in life, do not always come down to a simple either-or conclusion—even though there are plenty of bumper stickers and sermons that would have you believe that. Nor are there topics where you have to remain completely uneducated, because we are living in a time where there is more accessible information about any topic than there has ever been at any other point in history. And our written information is increasing exponentially every day.

If you are exploring new options, I hope that your default position is not to jump to the other side of the fence—as you will probably snag your crotch on the top while jumping over too quickly. Perhaps the words of Stephen Hawking will ring true on our approach to beliefs, as well as on anti-electrons: "If you meet with your antiself, do not shake hands; you would both vanish in a great flash of light."* While Hawking was not speaking about belief or disbelief, I think it is the natural inclination to jump to an opposite position when we are, for whatever reason, unsatisfied with our current position. Many of my classmates, when they started learning the history of the Bible and the small errors that have been introduced in it through the years, decided to view the Bible as completely made up and useless. Of course, this was their prerogative, but at that moment their belief-self and their belief-antiself shook hands and destroyed the faith that was there.

I hope I have suggested that there are other alternatives. Perhaps it is as easy as giving yourself a new title—just like the first followers of Jesus created their own label, "followers of the Way," while still living under the umbrella of Judaism and attending synagogues and going to the temple as they always had. In fact, before I landed on the label "hopeful skeptic," I tried on a couple others. The one I thought about the most was "a skeptic who tries to follow the teachings of Jesus," but that was quite bulky. Even though it felt bulky, though, it seemed to fit better than the label "Christian." I also tried "hopeful agnostic," but for the reasons I laid out earlier, *agnostic* has too much junk attached to it.

So my label morphed into "hopeful skeptic," a name that was honest about the two worlds that my beliefs simultaneously exist in. To call myself a skeptic would not have been a completely accurate description, because I am not skeptical of everything—nor am I a skeptic in the modern, rationalistic sense of the word. So I can't wear the label "skeptic" by itself. Nor would it have been totally accurate to label myself as an optimistic hopeful, because I don't rely completely on faith; I do bring a rationalistic and skeptical view to some of my theology.

But by using a somewhat creative label, I try to bring together the two worlds that I live between. The whole idea isn't about which part

---

*Stephen Hawking, *The Illustrated: A Brief History of Time* (London: Bantam, 1996), pp. 89-90.

of your mind to favor or whether to favor tradition versus new ideas. For me, the hopeful doesn't battle the skeptical. I don't turn everything into being either-or; I let the two exist and interact. Some people think it is *either* faith (hopefulness) *or* human understanding (skepticism), and that an individual has to choose one of the two. They don't like having the two under the same roof, and they think human understanding is flawed and should not be allowed to weigh in on matters of faith. But I like having them both as companions, each informing the other. So while I can understand these other people's position and I also understand how I fall outside of their categories, I just choose to take a different label, which helps foster some great conversations. I hope not to offend people who are inside preexisting labels because I'm not claiming to wear their nametags.

So if you feel completely bothered by an arranged marriage of faith and want to explore your own beliefs, I would suggest taking the time to create a title that accurately describes you—even if it isn't one that you are completely comfortable using in public. Perhaps a change in name would be all you need to get into a belief structure that fits you a little better, and maybe this small change would be enough to keep you as part of some sort of faith community without being against communities of faith as a whole.

You will have to search through your own house or apartment and work through your beliefs. It is probably something that you will do from time to time. And while going through those beliefs, there may be some that you want to get rid of and some that you know you want to keep. You may even find yourself investing in a label maker so you can work through the ones that will get boxed up.

NICE T-SHIRT, THEY ROCK

If you are into music, to the extent that you get merchandise from your favorite bands, maybe you have had the following experience. Perhaps you bought a concert T-shirt or even a shirt with a band's name or picture on it, and sometime after the purchase you are wearing your new fan gear, and then you've gotten criticized by a so-called diehard fan—saying that you can't *really* be a true fan of the band you are displaying.

This has happened to me occasionally. I love classic rock and used to wear a couple T-shirts from bands that were playing music before I was born. I would get chastised by some of the older crowd for not really being able to call myself a fan of the music because I wasn't there when it all happened. I am sure this happens to older people too when they wear concert T-shirts of new music, and it happens when anyone who is too preppy, too emo, too metal or too whatever wears a concert shirt that some would say that person can't possibly be a fan of.

The same sort of thing could happen when you have friends over who are perusing your CD collection (or, in my case, my iPod playlist; I don't have compact discs) or your DVD collection; they might read one of the titles of the movies aloud with a confused or disapproving tone of voice. *"You* like *Donnie Darko?"* "What do *you* know about BTO?" "Springsteen's new CD? Are you kidding me?"

Yes, I do like *Donnie Darko,* and I do appreciate the musical stylings of the Bachman-Turner Overdrive, who take care of business better than most. And, you know what? The Boss is still kicking it hard, so back off.

Back to the subject of religion, I have felt like I have been wearing a Christian T-shirt my whole life, and for the last five years, other Christians have been approaching me and, for one reason or another, saying that I'm not a true fan. Perhaps it is because of my different taste in theology or maybe because I like beer or because I don't go to church buildings anymore. It could be because I love asking questions and am quite skeptical, or maybe because I don't like to rely 100 percent on faith.

One of two things happens when a person is constantly approached and accused of not being a fan of the band they are wearing—when a supposed compatriot challenges your allegiance: (1) either you dig in and stand your ground, ever ready for that battle to show your true colors with a supposed fanmate and make a case that you support the artist (a choice that many brave souls are fighting for their bands or their titles), or (2) you start to realize that you don't really want to fight a constant battle of fandom, realizing that the army inspired by the band is very much different than you are, and perhaps you don't want to brandish their label anymore.

Perhaps the latter happens, and you think that the ethos of that crowd and those who spend their time and money on the merchandise and branding aren't like you at all. You still love the music, have the CDs and have attended some of the shows, but you distance yourself from the rest of the branded community. So you tuck away the concert T-shirt. But then you start to put up a flag to search for others like you. You tag music you like on your Facebook profile, you add to that long online list of things that you like, you describe yourself quite a bit on those sidebars in your blog, and you search Blogger and Technorati for people who have tags that look like your tags. You even share your iTunes library and search other people's music lists to find people like you.

Many people like me are tired of fighting against friends or churches, so we have taken off the old concert T-shirts and put up flags to search for others. And many of us have found groups where we can be ourselves more fully and live a life that is more abundant and true to who we are. We have found places in groups online, in inner-city work projects, in small groups of larger churches, in families in our suburbs or apartment complexes; we have found places where we can be ourselves and grow into that abundant life that works to grasp the divine truth that has been given to humankind. Groups like these give me hope, and I spend a good bit of my life finding these places and plugging people into these places. I do this so other people don't shake hands with an antiversion of themselves, but rather get introduced to gatherings that can help them find the person that they are meant to be—not just the opposite of the person they were.

If you feel even a little bit like I do, rest assured that there are people like us all over the globe, and with the technological revolution and ever-growing lists of subcultures, there is a place for you to express yourself and work out your faith in a meaningful way. You don't have to drop your religion or even your labels to find these groups. But if dropping those things will help you, you should feel free to do that. Jesus never asked you to take on the label "Christian," he just asked that you follow him. He never told anyone that perfection or an inerrant belief structure was a prerequisite to take his path. In fact, he took on disciples who were in movements counter to what he wanted to establish, such as tax collectors and zealots, but he knew the kind of minds and hearts that he wanted around him.

GOING HOME

Just before Leslie and I headed home, after our fourteen months away, we stopped in London. On a Sunday we happened to stumble into an afternoon service at Westminster Abbey, and I used the time to reflect on the trip and my ideas of hopeful skepticism. I realized that our old apartment was empty and that I was going home to boxes to unpack and a new apartment to fill. I was sad that our traveling was coming to an end, but I knew there would be other trips.

I realized that as I'd been traveling and so skeptical about churches, I hadn't been to a church service in over a year. So I sat under the burning gaze of the bust of William Blake, and I listened to the service and the beautiful choir. I actively became part of a service that has been going on for over a thousand years. I read the welcome in the bulletin and saw that "seekers and doubters" are warmly welcomed. I assumed that would include the likes of a hopeful skeptic. I went on to read in the bulletin that the collection that would be taken would be equally divided between disabled children and the Abbey. It seemed like some of my skepticism was already being addressed in an old, high church.

I was left feeling hopeful: I was in a church that I gave a few bucks to, and I was heading back home to unpack and start again. I know that hopeful skepticism has shaped my worldview, but I also know there are more trips coming for Leslie and me. And I know I will be re-packing boxes. And I know that we all change.

Inspiration and Insights

Admittedly I am not coming up with my ideas in a vacuum, nor do I hijack someone else's ideas and try to sell them as my own, but I do try to read and form new ideas, stories and metaphors from those already existing around me. In an effort to give you some idea of what fuels me, as well as give credit to any inspirational juice I may have gleaned from other sources, here are some things I really dug while thinking about this book. They didn't form all my thoughts of hopeful skepticism, but they did keep me thinking in one way or another, providing some source of inspiration.

Audio

Bruce Springsteen, *We Shall Overcome: The Seeger Sessions,* compact disc, Columbia Records, ©1998, 2006.

The Cobalt Season, *In Search of a Unified Theory,* compact disc, The Cobalt Season, ©2007.

Jon Black, *Goodbye Golden Age,* compact disc, Rebuilt Records, ©2008.

Joseph Campbell, *The Power of Myth* (a set of interviews), compact disc, Highbridge Audio, ©2001.

Josh Ritter, *The Animal Years,* compact disc, Josh Ritter, ©2006.

Manchester Orchestra, *Let My Pride Be What's Left Behind EP,* compact disc, Sony Music Entertainment, ©2008.

The Nick and Josh Podcast <http://thenickandjoshpodcast.com>.

Speaking of Faith with Krista Tippett <http://speakingoffaith.publicradio.org>, radio show/podcast.

Video

Chocolat, DVD, directed by Lasse Hallström (Miramax Films, 2001). A movie about a community of hope built around chocolate.

The Fountain, DVD, directed by Darren Aronofsky (Warner Brothers Pictures, 2006). An excellent movie about death, metaphor and storytelling.

Pan's Labyrinth, DVD, directed by Guillermo del Toro (Tequila Gang, 2006). A great story about reality, imagination, faith and storytelling.

John Safran vs. God, DVD, directed by Craig Melville (Ghost Pictures, 2004). An Australian TV series on DVD, where John Safran tries on different religions.

Lectio

Dave Andrews, *Christi-Anarchy* (Oxford: Lion Publishing, 2001). A book about the possibility of a radical compassion through understanding the life of Jesus.

Bart D. Ehrman, *Misquoting Jesus* (San Francisco: HarperOne, 2005); and *Lost Christianities* (New York: Oxford University Press, 2007). Two books about how the Bible and Christianity changed over the ages.

Don Everts, *One Guy's Head Series* (Downers Grove, Ill.: IVP Books, 2008). A collection of books that uses people in our head as a metaphor for our thoughts.

Yann Martel, *The Life of Pi* (Orlando, Fla.: Mariner Books, 2004). A story about the power of stories.

Brian McLaren, *A Generous Orthodoxy* (Grand Rapids: Zondervan, 2004); and *The Secret Message of Jesus* (Nashville: Thomas Nelson, 2006). Two books that examine a different side of Christianity.

Doug Pagitt, *Preaching Re-Imagined* (Grand Rapids: Zondervan, 2005). An exploration of what church looks like when the pastor isn't the single voice in the community.

Peter Rollins, *How (Not) to Speak of God* (Brewster, Mass.: Paraclete Press, 2006). A philosopher's idea on faith and the lack of faith.

John Shelby Spong, *Jesus for the Non-Religious* (San Francisco: Harper-One, 2008). My favorite book for what it looks like to follow Jesus when you don't follow Christianity.

Confero

Emergent Village <www.emergentvillage.com>

Emerging Church, U.K. <www.emergingchurch.info>

Kiva <www.kiva.org>

The Ooze <www.theooze.com>

Open Source Theology <www.opensourcetheology.net>

About the Artist

Justin Banger is a part-time librarian, an illustrator, a painter and a printmaker. His art (some of which is featured in this book) embraces the understanding that a picture is a puzzle. Rather than merely drawing a recognizable image that depicts a blatant scene or idea, he draws to create tension and juxtaposition among elements. The result is images that are perplexing—demanding an interpretation without providing one. His work has been exhibited internationally. In 2008, his illustration of Phyllis Tickle's "cable of meaning" metaphor was published in her book *The Great Emergence* after first appearing on *The Nick and Josh Podcast*. He has a B.F.A in printmaking and painting from the University of Montevallo and is currently pursuing a master's degree in education. He and his wife live in Birmingham, Alabama, with their marvelous daughter. Find more images and information at www .justinbangerart.com and at justin-banger@mac.com.

LIKEWISE. *Go and do.*

A man comes across an ancient enemy, beaten and left for dead. He lifts the wounded man onto the back of a donkey and takes him to an inn to tend to the man's recovery. Jesus tells this story and instructs those who are listening to "go and do likewise."

Likewise books explore a compassionate, active faith lived out in real time. When we're skeptical about the status quo, Likewise books challenge us to create culture responsibly. When we're confused about who we are and what we're supposed to be doing, Likewise books help us listen for God's voice. When we're discouraged by the troubled world we've inherited, Likewise books encourage us to hold onto hope.

In this life we will face challenges that demand our response. Likewise books face those challenges with us so we can act on faith.

likewisebooks.com